Whole Bean
the
Marriage Blend

Coffee Conversation Secrets for Maintaining Successfully Thriving, and Loving Relationships

R.L. (Bobby) & Patricia A. Scott

Copyright © 2022 R.L. (Bobby) & Patricia A. Scott.

All Rights Reserved. This book contains material protected under International and Federal Copyright Laws and Treaties. Any unauthorized reprint or use of this material is prohibited. No part of this book may be reproduced or transmitted in any form or by any means, electronic or mechanical, including photocopying, recording, or by any information storage and retrieval system without express written permission from the author/publisher.

Paperback: 979-8-88583-062-1
Hardback: 979-8-88583-063-8
Ebook: 978-1-64085-000-2

Library of Congress Control Number: 2022907147

"Life is not measured by the number of breaths we take, but by the moments that take our breath away."
— Anonymous

Dedication

To our four amazing children: Dorjän Sharif,
Seneca Cheyne, Talitha Cumi, and Jonathan Lee

And to our three precious grandchildren:
Ashley Taylor, Chinja Lim Cho, and August Lee Alexander

These are our stories, and you are our greatest legacy.
We wanted to do what we wished your grandparents
had done and passed on to us

CONTENTS

Tribute xi
Preface xiii
Introduction xv

Part I: The Beginning Of Us:
High School - College - Pregnancy - Marriage

Chapter 1:   High School: Where Focus Goes
                Energy Flows 3
                First Kiss: Best house party ever! 5
                So, We Meet Again 7
                First Date 8
                It's Official, We're a Couple 11
                Monthly Anniversaries:
                    A Cause Set In Motion. 11
                Slow It Down...Maybe? 13

Chapter 2:	College: Long Distance Romance........ 15
	CoffeeConversation 18
Chapter 3:	Pregnancy: Shacking Up................ 20
	Lamaze & Basketball................ 23
Chapter 4:	Marriage: This Relationship Is Over...Or Not?..................... 25
	A Multitude of Counselors 27
	Child Focused 29
	Coffee Conversation................. 30
	Four Day Engagement............... 33
	The Wedding...................... 35

Part II: Honeymoon in Iran: The Marriage Revolution

Chapter 5:	Relocation: A New Season 41
Chapter 6:	Move #1: Culture Shock............... 43
	We Didn't Sign Up For This........... 45
Chapter 7:	Move #2: Now, This Is More Like It 47
	A Slice Of Italy..................... 48
Chapter 8:	Move #3: Feeling The Pressure 49
	What's In A Name................... 50
Chapter 9:	Move #4: Total Immersion 52
	The Face-off...................... 56
Chapter 10:	Move #5: Toy Furniture 59
Chapter 11:	Move #6: Back To City Life............. 61
	Ducks All Lined Up — Then Came Jesus................. 63

Chapter 12: Move #7: Returning To Western
           Society............................66
Chapter 13: Move #8: Strikes, Tragedy, and Transitions...70
           Grief and the Immortal 72
           The Honeymoon Is Over —
              It's Time To Go Home 73
           Counting Down 74
           The S*** Hits The Fan................75
           A Daring Escape 76
           A Life Held In Balance...............76
           What's Next?......................77
Chapter 14: Move #9: Evacuation 79
Chapter 15: Boomerang: Back to "The World" 83
           Athens...........................84
           Coffee Conversation.................85

Part III: The Coffeehouse Conversations

Chapter 16: Don't Just Eavesdrop, Join Us!...........89
Chapter 17: My Daddy's Cup.....................92
Chapter 18: Men & Shopping......................95
Chapter 19: Commit To Your Commitments 99
Chapter 20: To Covenant…Or Not.................103
Chapter 21: Let's Talk About Sex.................108
Chapter 22: Rebirth Of Inspiration................113

Part IV: Anniversaries: The Relationship Optimization Tool

Chapter 23: Monthly Celebrations:
          The Relationship Optimization Tool...... 117
              What Is Your 'State'? 118
Chapter 24: The 25th Wedding Anniversary 120
Chapter 25: The 26th Wedding Anniversary 122
              Coffee Conversation.................. 122
Chapter 26: Our 552nd MonthlyCoupleVersary....... 128

Part V: Relational Fissures: Moments of Crisis

Chapter 27: Enter stooping down 133
Chapter 28: Interrupting The Domino Effect 135
Chapter 29: The Storm: Marriage in Chaos 139
              The Reconstruction Period:
                Starting Over 139
              Putting On A Good Face 140
              Self Talk 140
Chapter 30: Deserts, Mountaintops, Peaks,
              and Valleys 142

Conclusion 145
Epilogue 149
The Authors 151

TRIBUTE

To the people who were so beautifully instrumental in our lives that have since transitioned into eternity. You remain forever in our hearts:

Mr. & Mrs. Jasper L. & Ella O. Scott, my parents
Mr. & Mrs. Moses W. & Cleopatra Ross, Tricia's parents
Mr. Russell Penn, our teacher, my friend, and mentor
Mr. Stilè Reaves, our wedding photographer, my mentor
The Rev. E. T. Randall (Crosby) Osborn, my cousin
Alphonso Pacheco Dorrello, our friend
And my brother, Jasper Scott, Jr. (Scotty)

PREFACE

اصفهان *Esfahan – Hotel Khoroush – Monday, 29 January 1979 – 3:50 PM IRST (Iran Standard Time)*

"Pacheco, what do you mean you shot him...in the face!?"

The news spread throughout the city like a raging wildfire; a foreigner shot an Iranian taxi driver. This "foreigner" was my oft·times hot-headed Cuban-American friend Alphonso Pacheco Dorrello. The shooting prompted a demonstration of thousands in the streets outside the Hotel Kourosh. This protest ignited a series of events that, over the next 10 hours, would trigger the Embassy's immediate evacuation of all U.S. government employees and their dependents and strongly urge Americans to leave Iran.

Pacheco and I had been together all day. I was with him in the taxi just a few minutes ago. How could something go so seriously wrong so quickly?

Coffee Conversation
*Arabica Coffeehouse – Shaker Square Cleveland, OH –
Wednesday, 1 January 1987*

Tricia: Due to our living in Iran, we experienced almost every challenge to staying married that a newlywed couple could endure.

Bobby: I know! So much life happened in such a short period. A whirlwind of events. It seemed more like years than just nine months. It's still hard to believe that I was actually a hostage. It got really crazy after Pacheco shot that taxi driver!

T: I wonder what happened to him?

B: I have no idea. Pacheco gave me his jewelry to send to his dad in New York before they took him. That was it; I haven't heard anything since.

T: He must have really trusted you. I can't imagine being in one of their prisons.

B: Well, he didn't have many options at that moment. He definitely didn't trust anyone else in the room.

T: So many people thought this revolution wouldn't last long at all

B: And it's still going on today.

INTRODUCTION

This book saved our marriage.

Well, truth be told, and the truth should always be told, our writing this book caused us to concentrate and analyze the things surrounding our relationship that were helping or hurting us. The truth is that we wrote it for ourselves, or at least it started that way. It was fate. The crowded coffee shop, the people sitting next to us listening to our conversation, then the thought: *"Don't Just Eavesdrop. Join Us!"*

Let me unpack this. Over the past 605 months, we've done a lot of work on our relationship. This means that we've also done (and continue to do) the work necessary to better develop ourselves as individuals. You have to be the best version of "You" possible to be the best version of "Us." The great American entrepreneur, author, and motivational speaker Jim Rohn used to say, "Don't wish it was easier; wish you were better. Don't wish for less problems; wish for more skills. Don't wish for less challenge; wish for more wisdom."

The sub-title suggests there are conversations to be found within these pages. These are the stories and discussions regarding the life and times of our relationship together. We believe that you will see yourselves and your relationships in our renditions. We hope to be a catalyst for healing from all the hurt, disappointments, and heartache of failed relationships, particularly marriages. The answers are within you; they have been there all the time.

I believe that God has commissioned us to do this, so here it is! We invite you to sit down and take some time to relax. Share this cup of Marriage Blend with us; have the conversations required to begin the healing process. Even better, discuss how you can continue to love each other and successfully thrive in your relationship together.

Let's continue the conversation. We would love to hear from you. www.TheCoffeeCouple.org

PART I
THE BEGINNING OF US:
HIGH SCHOOL - COLLEGE - PREGNANCY - MARRIAGE

CHAPTER 1
High School:
Where Focus Goes Energy Flows
Cleveland, OH – John Hay High School – October 1971

I met Patricia in high school; she was in her senior year; I was a junior. The funny thing is that I was not supposed to be at that school. The district changed zoning, and our house was seven houses inside the new border.

I would see her at the occasional student council meeting and sporting events. "A.B" was her very cool varsity cheerleading nickname. She was petite with exotically attractive facial features. Still, she did not garner my full attention until an incident one afternoon after school. My best friend Ronnie Hodges and I were standing across from each other in the narrow doorway between the gymnasium and the cheerleader's room, waiting for the end of both practices. Our mutual and best friend Darryl Rugley played on the basketball team. Myrna Neal and Hazel Brown, Darryl and Ronnie's girlfriends, were cheerleaders.

As the cheerleaders passed us en route to the girls' locker room, we spoke to the girls we knew. Everyone returned our greetings, or at the very least responded positively; well, everyone except for this one "senior" cheerleader. We didn't know her, but I said hello, noticing how cute she looked in her form-fitting gym suit. She walked right past me as if I did not exist. Ronnie snickered and laughed at me. It was not that I was embarrassed, more like annoyed. Being ignored is one thing I cannot tolerate! I was laser-focused and determined to get past that aloof veneer; she would not dismiss me again. I did not have to wait long; the opportunity presented itself a few days later.

Patricia:

I have had hearing problems most of my life. I honestly did not hear Robert when he spoke to me outside the gym door. Plus, I did not find it particularly attractive for guys hanging around and making catcalling comments to cheerleaders.

I only knew Robert through references and a brief student council meeting. He had a reputation for being one of the fastest typists in the state. Several girls in my stenography class talked about his challenge to race anyone in typing. Personally, I thought it odd that a guy even liked typing, let alone was fast at it. I was a speed typist myself, but I did not feel the need to challenge him. Our subsequent encounter was at a student council meeting. He was president of one of the committees, but his presentation was on topics I was not interested in; still, I enjoyed the energetic way he shared. I found that energy attractive. I also knew he was vice president of the booster club. That was about all I knew about this "Junior."

First Kiss: *Best house party ever!*
Cleveland, OH – Stephanie Garland's house – Friday, 22 October 1971

The Autumn chill was perfect for the Friday night high school games and the house parties that followed. The most popular was at Stephanie's house, a 21 bedroom estate in Cleveland's historical Hough neighborhood. This area gained national attention from the 1966 race riots. I was one of the first people to arrive that night. I saw one of my classmates, she looked cute that night, so I made my way over to her. I was a good dancer and especially enjoyed the close embrace of slow dancing, so while we were dancing, I kissed her. It was like kissing a fish; I lost all interest.

A little while later, I spotted Patricia from across the crowded room. She looked good, wearing a black leather jacket over her cheerleader uniform. She still had that certain air of confidence and sophistication that I found very alluring but frustrating. Here was my opportunity to rectify being ignored at school, but before I could ask her to dance, she disappeared, probably going to another party; I hoped she would return.

About an hour later, she came back. I saw her heading into the kitchen with Stephanie. Here was the chance to make my move. I asked the DJ to play the newly released single by Michael Jackson, "Got To Be There." I went through the narrow hallway, past the broad staircase to the kitchen, to ask her to dance; she said yes. She had indeed gone to another party and seemed a little bit tipsy. The music started while still in the dark and secluded hallway. Seizing the moment, I embraced her, and we danced right there. It was magical as she melted into my arms. As the song ended, we held our close embrace while looking into each other's eyes, and then…, we kissed; our first kiss…., Her lips were so subtle, so soft.

That first kiss represented a personal victory for me. The incident at school had focused my attention on Patricia; now, she was in my arms. But it proved to be so much more. This is similar to the ecstatic moment of the American sailor kissing the nurse portrayed in Alfred Eisenstaedt's iconic photo: "V-J Day in Times Square." Or Gustav Klimt's masterpiece: "The Kiss."

If it is true that "Life is an Art Form," then the brush that we have used to paint our lives together has been the caress of our lips as we touch in a kiss. We did not return to the party. We spent the rest of the evening sitting outside on the front stoop, talking, waiting for my older brother to pick me up. I made up a farce about going to Detroit with him to take care of some business. I was embarrassed to tell her I had to get home before my curfew.

> **Secret:** *"Fortis Fortuna Adiuvat"*
> *(Fortune Favors the Bold)*

Patricia:

My friend Stephanie had the best parties in that big old house on E. 93rd. Her mom was also very cool. I went to her party first, then left with some friends to go to another one a few blocks away for a family member of one of my friends. They were serving alcohol in those infamous red plastic cups. We shared a cup on the way back to Stephanie's. It looked like the party was starting to thin out, so I went into the kitchen to hang out with her. I loved the homey spacious kitchen. While we were talking, Robert came into the kitchen and asked me to dance.

I said yes. I figured just one last dance before heading home; I live just down the street. Instead of going back to the living room, we began dancing in the hallway outside the kitchen. Have you ever had one of those moments where the world around you stopped? That was that moment for me. The song "Got to be There" by Michael Jackson was playing, and the dimly lit hallway made everything else disappear. We danced, then kissed. I did not even think about it. It just happened. It was good. It was the first of many kisses to come. I remember Stephanie making a playful comment as she walked past us.

After talking briefly, we went out to the front stoop to wait for his brother to pick him up. He said they were going out of town for the weekend, so I did not expect to talk with him anytime soon. We sat and talked for a while. I do not recall the conversation, but I remember how comfortable I was with him. It was like we had been friends all along.

So, We Meet Again
Cleveland, OH - McDonald's Restaurant - Thursday, 28 October 1971

We dubbed ourselves "The Triumphant Trio," Rob, Ron, and Rug, short for Robert, Ronnie, and Rugley. We were inseparable in those days. We were planning a Halloween party at Stephanie's house the coming Saturday. It was going to be epic! Patricia walked past our table while we were planning the party. We had not seen or talked with each other since our kiss. I left after her to ask her to come to the party with me. I caught up with her outside the restaurant and asked if I could walk her home. She agreed to be my date. We established the time I would pick her up for the party, then I left to catch up with my guys. I never made it to her house.

Patricia:

Robert and I did not speak to each other for almost a week after the party. I stopped in the McDonald's for a snack to eat for my walk home from school. I noticed Robert and his two friends sitting in a booth to my right towards the exit. I just glanced and smiled at him, but I did not stop. I could sense a commotion as I continued on my way out the door. He caught up with me at the traffic light and wanted to walk me home the rest of the way. After walking about a block, he asked me if I would go with him to a Halloween party at Stephanie's house that weekend. I said I would, and then we exchanged phone numbers.

During our walk, he seemed shy, nothing like the person I saw in the student council meeting or the person who came and grabbed me at the party to dance and kissed me. After I answered him, he abruptly turned on his heels, said goodbye, and ran off back in the direction of McDonald's. He never finished walking me home. I thought it was very amusing and laughed aloud as he ran off. I just stood there on Chester Avenue by the Call and Post Newspaper building and watched him, thinking he was excited about telling his friends I had said yes to the date.

First Date
Cleveland, OH - Saturday, 30 October 1971

Patricia:

On the evening of the party, Robert came to my house to pick me up. He walked into my backyard wearing a knit gray and burgundy shirt with blue jeans. His afro was neat and crowned his face nicely. I remember thinking that he looked cute and sexy. Funny, I have only thought of one other person in that way, and we never even kissed.

Robert:

I was excited. Stephanie's house was a popular party venue, and we had planned a few "haunting surprises" for our guests. Still, I was most excited because this would be my first date with Patricia. We had not spent much time together, and I would have an extra hour out because the clocks fall back with the end of daylight saving time.

Patricia lived down the street from Stephanie. It was a neat, well-kept little house. I noticed the well-appointed yard furniture, a large brick barbecue grill, and the dog barking at me as I approached her backyard. His name was Red, but she called him "Sugar." I liked how she said it, so I eventually stole that name for myself. She wore a cream and orange knit pants suit that nicely accentuated her petite and shapely body. Her exotic facial features were stunning; high cheekbones highlighting full subtle lips, lovely long hair, and bright, intelligent eyes.

Our haunted basement was an epic success. Several people were frightened by our antics until someone recognized my very distinctive laugh. The illusion was over, and the evening segued into a regular party. Patricia and I danced a couple of times in the grand party room before isolating ourselves in the more private cozy, dimly lit sunroom. One of Patricia's senior classmates, Norman Coffer, interrupted us twice, asking her to come back to the party and dance with him. He had a mad crush on her. I was glad that she turned him down and stayed with me.

I had no intention of asking Patricia to be my girlfriend that night; the timing was right; it felt good and genuine just being together. We went outside to the back stoop; it was spontaneous, intuitive, natural; I looked up at her from the lower step and asked her if she would "go with me?" (a colloquialism for dating exclusively) She paused, then said that she would "let me know." Not quite the reply that I expected. The rest of the evening was a blur for me. I knew it was going to be a long weekend.

Patricia:

After the basement haunting, Robert and I spent most of the night in the parlor next to the main party room. There were a couple of benches and a large U-shaped bar. Still hearing the music, we danced, talked, and kissed for the rest of the evening. Norman came to the door twice and asked me to dance; he was a classmate I had gone out with; I declined and stayed in the parlor. Then Robert escorted me outside to the back stoop, where we continued our conversation. We never strained to talk with one another. Whenever we were together, it just felt right. After talking about our families and school, he asked me to be his girlfriend. I was not surprised by the question but felt an answer warranted more time. I said I would let him know. It was not my intention to be exclusive with anyone at that time. I was seriously focused on my senior year and had already turned down two other guys' requests. I do not remember even thinking about how I would answer him. I figured I would just let time pass and see what would come of it.

After Robert left the party, I joined Stephanie in the kitchen. I figured I could stay out a little later, given the clocks turned back that night. I was so surprised when my mom showed up at the door looking for me. The short walk home should have been painful listening to her complaints about my poor decision to stay out late. But for some reason, it did not bother me too much. I had enjoyed my night, and nothing could take away from that fun time.

It's Official, We're a Couple
Cleveland, OH - John Hay High School - Tuesday, 2 November 1971

On Saturday night, I asked her to be my girlfriend; today was Tuesday, and I still had no answer. After school, we met at the bottom of the wide staircase in the basement, a short distance from the gym door where she had previously ignored me when I spoke to her. When pressed for an answer, she just said, "You already know." I took that response as a Yes!

We were the typical high school couple just getting to know each other. Not having any classes together limited our contact to before and after school. In the morning, we would rendezvous in the lower auditorium. From there, we moved to our secluded spot in the small doorway exit to the girls' locker room, making out until the first bell. We did a lot of kissing.

Monthly Anniversaries: A Cause Set In Motion
Cleveland, OH - John Hay High School - December 1971

As we approached our first month together, I heard that Michael Wilkerson and Norman Coffer intended to ask Patricia to her senior prom. They were both seniors and had access to cars; Wilkerson even rode a motorcycle! My confidence waned, and my adolescent 16-year-old mind was thinking, "why would this gorgeous senior cheerleader want to be escorted to her prom by a junior?" I figured that whatever perfectly aligned stars resulted in her being my girlfriend wouldn't last the next six months until prom.

I had a brilliant idea. It was our first month as a couple, and I wanted Patricia's mind on me, on us, all day long. I decided to write little notes and put them in her locker or desk before every class. Stuff such as: "Happy 1st Month Anniversary" or "Let's do something special after school." It was as if I was marking my territory.

I felt good about my ingenuity and creativity, well, at least until the 7th period. There was no response from Patricia; nothing. Two more periods left, and the school day was over. I began envisioning myself in the stands at the Friday game, watching all the cheerleaders reading my corney notes, pointing and laughing at me to scorn. I could not handle that level of embarrassment, so I concocted another plan. I would miss my next class, go to the counselor's office, and request an immediate transfer to another school. I would make up some plausible excuse to tell my parents when I got home. At the very least, I would not be coming to school the next day, thus breaking my perfect attendance record. And I definitely was not going to the game.

I was heading to the office when I saw Patricia coming toward me, and she was moving fast. I think it's over, I'm done for; she is not waiting until Friday. I am about to get embarrassed right here in the hallway. She walked up to me, stuffing a note in my hand while giving me a kiss on the cheek, saying to me, "You know I'm a senior and extremely busy, but I loved your notes." I do not remember what she said after that; I just stood in the hallway watching her rush off to her 8th-period class, thinking, "Well, that worked; I'm going to keep doing this!". In those few moments, I had gone from the depths of depression to the heights of euphoria. The movie "Titanic" did not exist until 1997, but I felt like the character Jack Dawson standing at the ship's bow exclaiming, "I'm the king of the world!"

I don't think I will ever forget that first month. Practically every month since, we have celebrated our relationship in some way. We have exchanged love notes, greeting cards, written letters, and given gifts. Sometimes, we just hung out, enjoying each other's company. At first, it was fun just adding up the months when so many high school romances just faded away. We had no idea of the enormous benefits celebrating our relationship every month would bring over the years.

Slow It Down...*Maybe?*
Cleveland, OH - John Hay High School - March 1972

Patricia:

As much as I enjoyed the attention, the many notes, and our walks at the Wade Oval lagoon, I grew increasingly aware that this was getting really serious.

I am on his mind. His many notes tell me I am a constant thought. These many letters reveal that this is more than being about a prom date. Even in the early stages of our relationship, writing to each other created a connection. One that flowed through every word in every letter. Soon, not getting a note would stir up a fear that something in our relationship was off. So we wrote to stay connected.

The seriousness of our relationship was a little frightening to me. I was not ready to fall in love, yet it was happening. It seemed entirely out of my control, so I had to roll with it and see if the relationship could stand me. I even tried sabotaging it by avoiding Robert for a bit to see if he would take the hint. It didn't take long for him to call me on it. We just seemed to be inevitable.

Self-sabotaging a relationship can have deep roots. I felt I had good reasons to avoid intimacy in the short term because of my long-term goals. I wanted the security I thought my future plans would bring me. I realized that it wasn't fair to not disclose my reasons to Robert, so I opened up. I was trying to avoid the emotions of pain and hurt if I got in too deep. It was not good to ignore my feelings, not the ones I had for him, nor the feelings I had about thoughts of abandoning my dreams. I felt that any future relationships would interfere with my plans. So, I decided to live in the present emotionally and was relieved after opening up.

> ***Secret:*** *If you find it challenging to open up and build intimacy in a relationship, examine your motives and look for any reasons you might be self-sabotaging. Being vulnerable to another human being isn't easy if you have past hurts or trauma. Give yourself permission to acknowledge that, and if you find you are in a pattern of ruining relationships, do the work to find out why. Self-sabotaging behaviors can develop long-term intimacy problems in relationships.*

CHAPTER 2
College: *Long Distance Romance*
Athens, OH - Ohio University - 1973-74

Bobby:

Fridays 3:00 PM ignited a mad rush of employees leaving the enormous Jones & Laughlin Steel Mill parking lot for a weekend of partying and relaxation. I will be spending the weekend on campus with Tricia. My packed bags were waiting in the car, ready for the 3 ½ hour drive to Ohio University in Athens, Ohio. We squeezed every minute possible out of those weekends. Many times I wouldn't leave the campus until late Sunday night. I was still living with my folks, and my mom told me that she got worried when she didn't hear from me all weekend. I was so excited about seeing Tricia that I forgot to let her know.

Our initial plan was to work over the summer after I graduated from high school and join Tricia in her sophomore year in the fall. She would earn her degree in journalism, and I would be studying photography and business. As the saying goes, "the best-laid plans of mice and men…," those plans never materialized. We did not receive any financial support from our families. After high school, Trica had to extend her summer job to work the entire year to save money and declare herself an independent student. Her folks refused to sign the financial aid forms to not divulge their personal business.

My Dad only completed the 8th grade and did not see a great need to pay for higher education. America was still in the "Golden Age" of manufacturing and industry, so well-paying jobs were plentiful with just a high school diploma. Following Tricia's lead, I also took a gap year to work and save for college.

Tricia went to school in the fall, but I kept working. I spent a lot of money on travel expenses and long-distance phone calls during that year. We wrote a lot of letters. I was so proud of her. She had a stellar first year, making the Dean's List even while working on campus and volunteering at the mental hospital.

Tricia:

You know you are really in love when your paradigm and vocabulary shift from "me, my and mine" to "you, us, and ours." We had trust in our relationship. We valued our time together and apart. Do I believe that our relationship would have survived my being away from school and Bobby in Cleveland? I have to say that I did. I think we would have had additional trials to work through, but I believe we would have done so. We made time for one another. Even though we did not have the technology available today that would have made staying connected so much easier.

The real reason I did not return to school was that Bobby would not be there. Just the thought of another year at Ohio University with him in Cleveland was disheartening. He traveled as often as he could to see me, and we talked on the phone for hours; still, the distance was too much for me. I sacrificed not going back to college to be closer to him. I did not believe that we were growing apart; I just missed being with him every day. I could have easily found the money to go back to school. I worked in the financial aid office. I just couldn't find the money for Bobby to come; he hadn't saved much; I suppose those phone bills and gas didn't help. We could have used some guidance at this point. If I had returned to school right away, there would not have been a 14-year gap before I resumed and earned my degree. We make choices. We should never blame our spouses or those we are in a relationship with for our decisions.

Our relationship lasted through my first year at college because we kept communications going. We did a lot of old-fashioned letter writing. I did not assume that there would be infidelity because of the distance. I remember how light I would feel the week before Bobby would drive down. The expectancy alone would get me through whatever was going on that week with school and work. We usually worked it out when we argued or fought, even long-distance. One time during an argument, I just hung up the phone. Bobby was so mad that he appeared at my dorm room door a couple of hours later. He said, "don't you ever hang up on me again," and turned to leave, presumably driving back to Cleveland.

CoffeeConversation
South Euclid, OH – Kitchen Table – July 2015 10 AM EDT

Tricia: Bobby, most of the time, I was like...even in high school, I was like, I don't know, I didn't want to be bothered, boys were a distraction to me.

Bobby: You sound like Seneca (our son), not wanting the distraction of a serious relationship.

T: Yeah, they are distracting. I mean, I wasn't looking for a man! I wasn't looking for a boyfriend; I really wasn't...

B: That's true

T: Far from it, I had other stuff on my brain, and it wasn't that! (chuckles)

B: So, I was just a distraction then?

T: Uh uh, you were. You were a distraction in college, and then when you weren't coming to O.U., it was like a big distraction. I didn't go back to school in September because you didn't come.

B: But you didn't go anywhere else.

T: No, I didn't; I made a decision, I came back home, and I went back to work

B: Yeah, to make more money

T: Right

B: It was out of funding, also

T: Yeah, some of it was because the money I had saved I gave to my dad

B: Yeah

T: Who didn't give it back, and I didn't have the money that I once had

B: And the financial aid check that came in for you, he used that also

T: Right, I didn't have the money that I once had, so, you know, that was a financial decision as well...so

B: It was ...

CHAPTER 3
Pregnancy: *Shacking Up*
Cleveland, OH – Diana Lee Apartments – March 1975

Bobby:

We were very young and very much in love. Even though we took precautions, our first child was on the way. Well, so much for our intricately planned future. Pregnant; now there's a life interruption for you. We suddenly had some big decisions to make. Fortunately, we decided to accept responsibility for our actions. Abortion was not widely popular or readily available in 1974, and it was never a viable option for us because of our love and respect for the life we had created. I continued working at the steel mill; Tricia postponed going back to college until the baby was of school age. There would be three more babies and 14 years before she would return.

I found it ironic that Tricia's parents tripped out when we told them that she was pregnant and we were getting an apartment. Especially since their marriage and business were dubious at best, her mom said we just wanted to "shack up." In retrospect, I think they were in shock. Tricia was their oldest child, and she had a lot of responsibilities in the household, practically raising her younger siblings. People tend to say hurtful things when camouflaging their shock and disappointment.

Finding an apartment in a good neighborhood that accepted unmarried couples was quite an undertaking. Back then, society frowned on couples living outside the conventional norm of marriage. It felt like we were on a treadmill, having to run hard just to keep up with all the issues coming at us. I remember the first time shopping with Tricia to get groceries and the staples needed to set up our new home. I felt like I had no control over my money. They were just taking it out of my pocket! What items do you put back? Do we really need all of this stuff?

Tricia:

This will probably be the most challenging section for me to write. People have diverse ideas and beliefs about what marriage is. Our concepts on this subject will no doubt be challenged and even attacked. These beliefs have given us the marriage we enjoy today. As a Christian couple, the experience we share gives us a forever blessing—God is in our union.

When I look at why people live together and never commit to marriage, I have to be open and listen to why they make that decision. When Bobby and I decided to live together and not marry, I was pregnant and expecting our first child. We were young and in love. We wanted, like any parent, what would be the best for our child. We were not prepared, but what in life are we really totally prepared for? Even when you think you have things figured out, life can throw you a curve. I was ready to commit to a marriage relationship. Bobby, I believe, was not. I just felt that marriage would eventually come.

The world was becoming more open to partners living together and raising children without being married. I grew up with the stigma of having a "bastard child." Much of my thinking around marriage was to avoid that stigma. I really didn't know why being married would be different from "shacking up," as they used to call it. I just felt deep down inside that there should be a difference. My parents, as far as I knew, were never officially married. I always felt a void because of this. There was something that was missing. I know they truly loved one another.

> **Secret:** *First of all, you stand up. Take responsibility for your actions. If you are grown enough to make a baby, then be man and woman enough to accept the consequences of your actions. People say, "if I could do it all over again, I wouldn't change a thing." Well, that's just a load of crap. Of course, you would do it differently. That doesn't mean you don't love your kids and how your life has turned out. If we hold on to that opinion, what philosophy do we teach our children? That it's ok to make the same mistakes we did because it turned out alright? No way! If you break the rules and make some mistakes (which we all do), then own up to them and point the next generation to a better way.*

Lamaze & Basketball

Tricia decided to use the Lamaze method of childbirth. I thought it avant-garde but fully trusted her wisdom. She found a registered nurse who was a Lamaze Certified Childbirth Educator. She held classes privately in her home.

My involvement would be to drop her off and pick her up on time. Well, that was old-school thinking on my part when men's involvement with childbirth started and stopped in the waiting room. I was on my way to play some basketball. I had on my gear, and the ball was in the car. It goes to a young mindset concerning shared responsibilities and ownership. Of course, I ended up at the Lamaze class (in my basketball gear) right where I should have been, and I was ultimately a better father for it!

Tricia:

There was a time when the birthing process was left to the mother, midwife, or doctor. Fathers were left waiting in the wings. The culture had become more open to fathers having a more active role. My doctor accepted Bobby being in the delivery room as long as he didn't get in the way; I felt the Lamaze class would give him the information he needed to prepare for the experience.

It never occurred to me that Bobby would drop me off and play basketball. I was taken aback, but I remember sitting in the car discussing his purpose and being present, now and at the birth. He just hadn't thought it through. Nonetheless, we both experienced that first class together. It was fun for him and informative. He never missed a session, and he was a great Lamaze coach. He even had a t-shirt that said "Coach" on it.

Dorjän's birth was the most difficult of any of my pregnancies. The doctor was advising a C-section. Bobby's presence and that Lamaze class helped me decide not to. I'm grateful that we were empowered with the knowledge and tools we needed at that moment to work together for a good outcome and no C-section.

CHAPTER 4
Marriage: *This Relationship Is Over...Or Not?*

Bedford Heights, OH - Bear Creek Village - Tuesday, 28 March 1978

We had been together for six years and four months; now, it was over. Tricia told me that if we were not going to the next level, she was moving on, relocating to New England with Dorjän to finish her degree. So we were processing our amicable breakup. We had busy lives, both working full and part-time jobs. I also did freelance photography while attending art school and community college. My plan was to continue everything I was already doing while living "the ultimate bachelor's life." A Yiddish proverb says, "Der mentsh trakht un got lakht," translated "Man plans and God laughs."

During this transitional time, my oldest brother Jasper (Scotty) and his family were heading to the Middle East for his new job with Bell Helicopter International (Bell). I envied his lucrative and exciting opportunity. Scotty phoned me from Texas, informing me they needed one more photographer for Iran, and am I interested? ...Yes! Working as a photographer living abroad was my dream job! I had to be there by Monday at my own expense. I was on the next thing flying out! I went out with Scotty and his old Air Force buddies. I tried to hang with them while drinking Scotch and milk, but I just ended up getting drunk.

The interview went well; they seemed impressed with my work and professionalism. Still, I figured it was a long shot with my limited experience. I returned home and continued my busy routine without further thought about it. I did not want to get my hopes up.

It had been a week since the interview. After work, I sat in front of the apartment talking on the CB (Citizen Band) radio. Like most days lately, I was in no hurry to go inside or intend on staying long. Tricia held up the phone and knocked on the window to get my attention. Bell was on the line offering me the job. It was a 3-year contract, an impressive salary, with an additional housing stipend. This changes everything! Iran is over 6,000 miles away, and they wanted me there in two weeks! Going to New England was an easy 10-12 hour drive, one I planned on taking often. I still loved Tricia and completely adored my son despite our breaking up. Moving to the Middle East was another matter entirely. Here is where "God laughed" at my plans.

What to do, what to do? It was 1978; no internet, Skype, Zoom, or social media were available. The only options were expensive long-distance phone calls and regular "snail mail." It could be six months between visits. Instinctively, I knew that this was a significant decision, and I had to make it right away. I have always benefited from the wisdom and counsel of older men, and I desperately needed advice and directions, so I went to see my Dad.

A Multitude of Counselors

Discussions of this magnitude warranted the sanctum of his bedroom office. Dad listened as I explained the situation, then he paused in reflection. He told me that he liked Patricia and that she was a "good catch." His advice was to marry and that "A man could have his cake and eat it too." I have to admit that I was perplexed and a little shocked at this cavalier approach to marriage. I did not expect that! After telling him that I appreciated his advice, I left, still wavering. I needed to talk to Russ. Russ Penn was our former high school math teacher. He retired from education after his wife passed away from cancer. Our lives crossed again when he was prospecting former students for Penn Mutual Insurance Company. (I thought the name was quite a coincidence) He sold us our first life insurance policy. For some reason, he and I just hit it off and began spending a lot of time together hanging out and smoking weed. He had become my friend and confidant.

This was an entirely different type of conversation. Russ listened patiently to my trepidation about moving so far away, to my indecisiveness and excessive rambling. Suddenly, he slammed the palm of his hand on the wooden dining room table — The booming sound seemed to reverberate through my chest, stopping me dead in my tracks. Looking straight into my eyes, he said, "Scott, do you love the girl?" Stripped bare, I had nothing to say but a resounding "Yes; Yes I do!" Everything became crystal clear. I made my decision. Excited, I had to get an engagement ring right away and ask Tricia to marry me. Russ told me not to worry about that stuff, just go home. I left there with a made-up and determined mind, making a beeline for our apartment and my destiny.

It was Tuesday night. Our wedding was the following Sunday afternoon at my parents' house.

> **Secret:** *Make a Decision. Nothing happens until you decide instead of wavering between opinions. Decisions lead you to take action. Indecisiveness stagnates, and the opportunity might just pass you by. Seek wise counsel, always have mentors.*

Tricia:

Wow, that could have all turned out so differently. I could have threatened Bobby with not being able to see his son. Called it abandonment. He could have done the same with me if I had taken Dorjän to another state; it would have been a fight. But we didn't do that. Why? I believe we each had the other's best interests at heart. I was willing to let him go, and he was ready to do the same with me. That old saying, "If you love something, set it free. If it comes back, it's yours. If not, it was never meant to be"—Richard Bach. This was true for us.

I have to ponder what it would have been like had I said no to his marriage proposal. Would he have really stayed overseas for the entire time without seeing Dorjän, or would he have returned to the States? Guess we'll never know.

Child Focused
Richmond Heights, OH - Richmond Place Condominiums - April 2020

Tricia:

We should never use children as leverage. Using children to influence or manipulate another person in a relationship is damaging and cruel. We have the responsibility to act on behalf of children. Your feelings about a spouse or partner are your own. Trying to gain power by using children is emotional abuse. Unreasonable demands placed on children to coerce a partner only lead to bad outcomes and toxic conditions that can lead to anxiety, depression, and fear in children.

Children change the landscape of a relationship. The family structure is so critical to the development of a child. It takes committed parents who can work on their problems with their partners in progressive and healthy ways. This example teaches children how to resolve conflicts and makes them feel secure. As a teacher, I have heard the heart cries of children who were pawns in their parents' war. It is painful.

Children make us want to be better. When parents have their children's best interests as foundational, it draws them together in ways nothing else can. The ability to come together, make decisions, and share parenting is a pathway couples can use to solve problems in their relationship. I have seen parents who are successful at Cooperative Parenting. Still, they don't use these same strategies to improve their relationship. It is the agreement that is the key. Conflicts can be resolved once a couple decides to do the work. Suppose you can agree and work out how you will parent without the toxic dialogue and manipulative behavior. Why not use that same process to decide on other things as well? Good parenting takes good communication skills and discipline; both are important in an emotionally healthy relationship. Success in one area can lead to success in other areas.

Good parents teach their children how to trust, set boundaries, and resolve conflicts. These same strategies can help parents improve their interactions. The parents' resolve to co-parent effectively involves trust, commitment, and consistency. All are ideal beginnings that can enhance the adult relationship. Because a loving home with both parents is the very best foundation for children.

Coffee Conversation
South Euclid, OH - Kitchen Table - July 2015

Bobby: So here's my question. I want to know your thoughts or what you can recollect about our engagement?

Tricia: (poignant pause) O--kay.

B: I remember that you were on the phone with Bell right after I drove home from work that day, and that was when I got the job offer.

T: But then you left back out, and later you came in taking stuff out, your so-called "Little black books" and showing me everything like, "look, this is everything, this is all of it, I'm giving all this up, ok." You told me the conversations with your Dad and Russ, and that's when you decided you wanted to marry me

B: Yep, I was all in! I remember you also saying, "I don't need to see all of that"

T: Right, I did say that (chuckle) because I already knew. I mean, there was really nothing else; that was it. Then we proceeded to figure out how we were going to get married in just a few days (chuckle)

B: *So, ok, I left back out to go seek advice; I realized that this was a serious decision*

T: *Hm-Hmm (nodding in agreement)*

B: *It made me realize that I didn't want to split up. I think it was really one of those "God moments."*

T: *Hmmm (nodding in agreement)*

B: *So, what were your thoughts when you said yes?*

T: *I don't remember!*

B: *Try*

T: *Other than you finally came to your senses, I don't remember, I really don't. I might have felt that it was inevitable. It was not like a surprise that you would want to marry me, that didn't really surprise me, but...*

B: *When I left, you knew that I had this opportunity to move to Iran...*

T: *I was happy for you; I was. I was excited for you; It was a great opportunity. That was it. I didn't think about going with you or even being over there; I was moving on doing what I was doing, so that was it.*

B: *So you were in the process of putting in college applications and looking at apartments?*

T: *I would have been back home for awhile*

B: *You were thinking about moving back home?*

T: *Hm, I had to go back home before I went out*

B: *Really!*

T: *Yeah, that was March. I knew I wouldn't be moving until time to go to school in September. I had a few months* to plan and do what I needed to do. I would have been at home.

B: I didn't know you were planning on moving back home

T: Where else was I going to go?

B: I thought you were looking at getting a job and an apartment

T: Right, I was, ok, those things take time, looking at transferring jobs and.., I mean, but at that point it was... I've got to go back home, you got that job relatively quickly and had to make a decision. It wasn't like...

B: Yeah, they wanted me there in a couple of weeks

T: Right, we had started packing up, I think our lease was coming up, but we already knew we were going our separate ways

B: Well, the evening you said yes, we were officially engaged

T: Right.

B: I gave you that big ole engagement ring and everything, don't you remember that?

T: You didn't give me a ring. What are you talking about? We went and got wedding rings together.

B: I know we did (chuckling)

T: It was moving fast. We were at the point where you're going to have to decide; you either want me or you don't; that was my feeling. I already knew you were messing around

B: We were breaking up

T: Ok, so it was like, ok, you need to make a decision

B: You were playing with messing around

T: No, I was not

B: You had guys that wanted to go out with you

T: That doesn't mean I was playing with anything; they approached me; I wasn't looking for anybody else. I didn't want to be bothered; men are a distraction to me

B: Right, you've always said that

Four Day Engagement
Bedford Heights, OH – Bear Creek Village – Saturday, 1 April 1978

Bobby:

We did it; tomorrow was our wedding day! Getting married at my parents' house, where I grew up, was very special. We were young, in love, and determined, giving little or no thought to restrictions or limitations. We planned and executed our wedding in just four days with all the pomp and circumstance we could muster.

One of the biggest challenges to our short planning time was shooting Ervin and Silvia's wedding on Saturday. It was too late to cancel, and besides, they were friends of ours, so Tricia also attended. We got home well after midnight. We are both night owls, but the realization that our wedding was only a few hours away was starting to set in.

We accomplished a lot over the last 84 hours, but we still had those tedious last-minute preparations to complete. On edge and grumpier by the minute, I needed a break. We packed up, grabbed Dorjän and Tricia's sister Pam, and headed out to The Country Kitchen restaurant, our late-night breakfast spot. Replenished, we left the restaurant and took Pam home. By the time we got to my folks, I was wiped out. I remember listening to Tricia and my mom working in the kitchen as I fell off to sleep.

Tricia:

Your engagement is the most romantic. He had no engagement ring; it was not at Disney World or even over a fancy dinner. I have heard that about 61% of guys consult with their fiance before buying a ring. We bought our wedding rings together. We did not have social media, so neither of us could update our status, yet, there we were, about to change everything. We had to make a decision quickly. Life has a way of pressuring you to make decisions.

Our wedding date gave us little time to shop for rings, get a minister, and book a venue. Yet, the events of these few days are so vivid in my mind. Our day-to-day tasks left little room to think about ourselves as becoming Mr. and Mrs.

I imagine most women dream of a fairy tale wedding. I was no exception. That was not going to happen with only four days to plan. Somehow, we got it all done, and the big day arrived. Getting married on a Sunday was not common in the Black community.

Bobby had to shoot a wedding on Saturday that I would also be attending, so it was Sunday by default. Let's just say there was not much sleeping going on. My sister Pam was a tremendous help with watching Dorjän. My dearest soon-to-be mother-in-law, Madear, was so helpful. I suppose not many women can say they made their own wedding cake. I did, with Madear's help. I also helped my dad with the hors d'oeuvres we would serve after the ceremony.

The Wedding
Cleveland, OH – Sunday, 2 April 1978

It was 40° with a trace of snow, a perfect day for an early spring wedding in NE Ohio. I thought I was cool, calm, and collected. That was until I cut myself while trimming my face with scissors. Before getting dressed, my best man (and 'road dog') Romerio Moreno and I went outside to smoke a joint. I needed to take the edge off, relax and be in the moment.

We had a small wedding party of six. Dorjän was our ring bearer; Tricia's sisters, Pamela and Jacqueline, were her maid of honor and our flower girl. My mentor, Stilé Reaves, was our photographer. Tricia's dad catered, and my cousin, Rev. E. Randall T. Osborn (Crosby), officiated. This living room has seen many weddings, but ours will be the last one.

Crosby gave us some avant-garde vows, something about staying married as long as it was convenient. Tricia and I recited the traditional vows in our heads. I asked him about what he said afterward. He asked me, "wasn't I listening?" This was his typical challenging manner.

After the photos, we joined our guests for cake and light hors d'oeuvres in the dining room. Then off to the Front Row Theater with Romerio and his wedding date to see Rufus & Chaka Khan and Heatwave in concert. It is still hard to believe that we pulled this off in just four days!

We came back home to the same apartment, but something was different; something had definitely changed. We had transitioned to a new level in our relationship; the marriage covenant.

Tricia:

Ours was not the first wedding at Bobby's parents' house. It was beautiful being surrounded by family and close friends. I think having people we loved there to see us get married and see us off at the same time was very comforting to me.

My sisters were my bridesmaid and flower girl. Our two-year-old son, Dorjän, was our ring bearer. We both loved the wedding scene in Fiddler on the Roof, so "Sunrise Sunset" was our wedding march song. My processional began with my dad at the top of the narrow second-floor staircase. As we approached the landing, he asked me, "was I ready?"

As I walked toward Bobby and the minister, everyone pressed in to see my dad and me. I could feel the blessing, love, and energy in the room with every smile. We didn't write our own vows, and the words his cousin Rev. E. Randall T. Osburn spoke over us were very contemporary. But it didn't matter; in our hearts, we knew we wanted nothing less than an eternity together.

The reception was short because we were going to go to a concert. I felt a little sad knowing that it would be a while before I saw many of these family and friends again. To this day, I regret that I did not have a good picture of my wedding cake. I had put all my love and affection into that cake, and I hoped that everyone eating it would feel it.

The concert was fantastic, although the events of the prior days had worn Bobby down, and he slept through a great deal of it. The music of that concert would become part of the musical fabric of our lives.

Secret: *Project your future as best as you can. Predict multiple scenarios together and determine the desired outcomes. Plan the contingencies so that unexpected situations and emergencies don't catch you by surprise.*

Do you value the person and relationship so much that your future seems less without them?

Do you both see the other person as viable for your future?

Know and share your values.

PART II
HONEYMOON IN IRAN:
THE MARRIAGE REVOLUTION

CHAPTER 5
Relocation: A New Season
Cleveland, OH – April 1978

Bobby:

Those were exciting times! Leaving everything behind, we were embarking on a grand adventure to the other side of the world. Landing the position as a photographer for Bell Helicopter International (Bell) was a dream come true.

With our wedding firmly behind us, we had just a few more tasks to complete: passports, immunizations, voltage converter adapters, resigning from our jobs, etc. One of my most challenging tasks was selling my prized 1975 Limited Edition Pontiac Trans-Am. It was more than just a car for me; it anchored my identity! I looked into shipping but was not able to pull together the resources.

A few days later, we boarded our flight with a mixture of apprehension and excitement, a young newlywed couple with their 2-year-old son in tow. We purchased a ginormous

> *"Let others lead small lives, but not you. Let others argue over small things, but not you. Let others cry over small hurts, but not you. Let others leave their future in someone else's hands, but not you".*
> *Jim Rohn*

Pajama Teddy Bear to accompany Dorjän on the trip. It was bigger than he was!

Persians call Esfahan "Nesfe Jahan," which means "Half of the World." For the next three years, Iran was to be our new home, our entire world.

Tricia:

After only a four-day engagement and Sunday wedding at Bobby's parents' home, we headed to Esfahan, Iran. I entered into this new era in our relationship with excitement and anticipation. Our trip to Iran met with the same energy. I was eager to enter a new phase of my life as a wife and soon a visitor in a strange country.

My brain had no time to process everything because of my busyness. Closing up an apartment and planning a wedding was crowded with preparing to leave the country. We had to learn about the culture and laws of Iran. We had to get shots, passports, and medical records for ourselves and Dorjän. There were logistics to comply with for what belongings we could ship.

CHAPTER 6
Move #1: *Culture Shock*
Cleveland – Tehran – Esfahan

Tricia:

Our moving to Iran would start our married life together. It was our honeymoon destination, and it would be our new home. This would be the longest flight I have experienced. We left Texas for New York and then to Paris, where we had just an hour layover. There was not much to see at the airport, but unfortunately, we did not have enough time to go into the city. Exhaustion set in from the previous days' preparations, hustle, and bustle; then the travel and arrival in Tehran and the short plane shuttle to Esfahan. Our first few hours in Iran would affect Bobby and me much differently.

Bobby inadvertently gave a "thumbs up" to the Iranian men that helped with our luggage at the airport in Tehran, and he received very threatening glances that made him uneasy. We sat separately on the shuttle flight to Esfahan. The crowded plane was noisy; commuters sat doubled up, luggage on their laps. Dorjän and I sat on the right side of the aircraft and could see the view of the lights from the Azadi Tower. Bobby, seated on the opposite side, could see nothing more than the heads and backs of strangers. The short flight was turbulent, and I should have been frightened by it. Still, my excitement overrode any fear of the unknowns I was about to encounter. We arrived in Esfahan at about 9:30 that evening.

Bobby:

The flight to Tehran was long but comfortable. Everything went well until we boarded the plane in Tehran for the short flight to Esfahan. The Iranian baggage handlers were very helpful and efficient in loading our luggage into the small shuttle plane. I smiled, giving them an enthusiastic thumbs up; the American gesture of approval popularized by "The Fonz" on the TV show "Happy Days." Their response was entirely unexpected; they looked like they wanted to tear me apart. That caught me completely off guard and really shook me up. I would later discover that all upward hand gestures are considered insults in the Middle East. From their perspective, I had returned kindness with vulgarity. I was more determined than ever to learn about these people and their culture.

Midway through the flight, Tricia, Dorjän, and the other passengers were enthralled by seeing the lighting display from the Shah's Memorial Tower. I couldn't see a thing seated on the other side of the plane with a lap full of luggage next to the lady with a sheep on her lap. So.., I was threatened at the airport, then crammed into a seat next to livestock while missing the first unique sites of Iran. I am not a happy camper.

We Didn't Sign Up For This

Tricia:

Our first night in Esfahan would begin with a very short stay in the Isfahan Hotel, where Bobby showed signs of "what have I done?" Hotel standards are not the same all over the world. It was a small, shabby, and dim room. I prepared to get Dorjän ready for bed. We were thinking of sleeping in our clothes, ready to leave at a moment's notice. We were supposed to stay in this hotel for at least 45 days until our housing came through. I think that thought alone set Bobby in a panic. I was amazed by his diminished sense of adventure. After seeing 'the bug,' a size I had not encountered, he called his brother Scotty. We would not be staying here.

Bobby:

Frustrated and exhausted from travel, we finally arrived at the Isfahan Hotel. Bell had set up our lodging here for the 45-day orientation. The lobby was impressively large, ornate, and very Persian. But then we got to our room — Oh boy, talk about small and cramped. There was a standard-sized bed in the middle of a dimly lit room that would hardly accommodate the three of us, much less our luggage. No way we are staying in this place! I immediately got on the phone with my brother Scotty — who was my catalyst for getting this job.

    After letting him know we had safely arrived, I asked him to come and pick us up from this dump? The excitement had waned; we were all exhausted. We lay fully clothed on the bed until Scotty arrived. I told Tricia that I would figure out how to get us out of here and back home; this Middle

East thing is not working out. She just looked at me and chuckled at my pitifulness.

Scotty and his friend came to get us in a small pickup truck. Tricia rode in the front middle seat while Jacy (Dorjän's nickname) and I rode in the open cargo bed. It was well into the evening as we drove the short distance to the Suite Hotel where Scotty and his family were staying. The shops had reopened from the midday siesta. The kinetic energy of the city was tangible. The hustle and bustle of people and commerce, the sounds, the smell of grilled corn on the cob, that's when it hit me; this city was enchanting! We were going to be just fine here.

CHAPTER 7
Move #2: *Now, This Is More Like It*

Bobby:

The following day after securing the transfer of our lodging from the Isfahan Hotel to the Suite Hotel, Tricia and I began our exploration of this new city, its people, and its culture. Esfahan was beautiful! Wide tree-lined avenues bordered by canals called 'Jubes' on both sides. Across the street from our hotel was the Si-o-Se Pol (which means 33 in Farsi), or The "33 Arch Bridge,"; the longest and most lovely of the 11 bridges of Esfahan.

Esfahan is Iran's capital of culture and is beautiful in every season. One afternoon while walking across the bridge, a car pulled up to greet us with a hand extended from the passenger window. After shaking their hands, for the next 15 minutes, practically every vehicle crossing the bridge lined up to do the same. We felt like celebrities. This type of reception, mixed with curiosity, and friendliness, remained consistent for most of our time here.

Tricia:

We moved to the Suite Hotel, where Scotty and his family lived. We extended the 45 days of orientation, so this hotel was our home for almost two months. The owner was a French lady. Dorjän contracted measles while playing with her little girl. I quarantined him in our room until he was no longer contagious; I was the most lonely I had ever felt. I found myself looking forward to eleven o'clock when Sesame Street came on the television. The only thing in English we could watch. It gave Dorjän a distraction from the scratching and me some time to myself. My other reprieve was climbing out of our hotel room window onto the roof, where Dorjän and I could get some much-needed fresh air. I enjoyed the view of the city and watching people going out and returning from shopping. I could not wait to go out to the bazaars and markets to shop.

A Slice Of Italy

I remember the very moment I saw her. Tricia and I were sitting out front of the Suite Hotel. Suddenly, there she was: A red and flashy Fiat 128 SL, driven by a dashing young Iranian helicopter pilot, and she was for sale. Buying an Italian-made car in provincial Esfahan was an impetuous acquisition, not the best decision I've ever had. There was nowhere to get it worked on, no one to work on it, and all the parts had to come from Tehran via Italy. However, I was instantly and hopelessly emotionally attached, still regretting having to leave my cherished Trans-Am behind in the states. At this time, I knew nothing about Tarof تعارف; the Iranian art of negotiation and haggling, but in my defense, I was only 22 years old, and it was a very cool-looking car, so I bought it, but not at the best price.

CHAPTER 8
Move #3: *Feeling The Pressure*

Tricia:

After a couple of weeks, we moved to a more spacious suite, but it did not take away the loneliness I felt. Bobby was away for long hours each day. I had to wash clothes in the hotel tub and hang them around the room to dry. Dorjän could run around the hotel freely to play. Iranians loved children, especially boys, but this was no way for a two-year-old to live.

The pressure of finding housing, the long lonely days, and living conditions became too much for me. One day this led to a big argument between Bobby and me. Bobby slapped me. He shocked even himself. I immediately thought, "what have I done? Should I be here? Did this all happen too fast?" He was dreadfully sorry, and he apologized immediately and emphatically. Still, I knew right then that I would be gone if he ever did that again. He has never hit me again — Ever!

Bobby:

Our contract with Bell included an additional housing stipend after the orientation period in the hotel. There were no restrictions on where you lived as long as you got to work on time. Wanting to take advantage of this opportunity, we sought housing locations that would be fully immersed in the Iranian culture.

It took longer than we expected to find the housing we desired. We were granted an extension to our orientation period and moved to a more spacious and comfortable room at the hotel. The hotel was owned by a French woman whose daughter was the same age as our son. They became constant playmates. She spoke a mixture of French and Farsi, but they had no problem communicating.

What's In A Name

We chose the name "Dorjän" and the nickname "Jacy" from Sue Browder's "The New Age Baby Name Book." Born out of wedlock, we used Tricia's maiden name, Abernathy. After we married, we changed his full name to Dorjän Sharif Abernathy-Scott — which loosely translates to "Good and Honest Black man." When we chose his name, we had no idea that we would be living in the Middle East; it was just providence. Persian culture holds boys and men in high regard. When the men working at the hotel heard Dorjän's Arabic middle name, Sharif, they went crazy over him! They would pick him up and fuss over him every time we walked past the front desk.

Mansoor, one of the hotel clerks, was so enamored with us that he told everyone in his village about our little family. He told us that his grandmother was making a Persian rug for us, but it would take three years to complete. His village was famous for these expensive Iranian carpets, which we would surely treasure.

CHAPTER 9
Move #4: *Total Immersion*

Tricia:

Finally, we found a place in which to live. It was a cluster of brand new villas in a rural village called Homayunshahr, located 25 minutes from Esfahan. Bobby's brother Scotty, his wife Marilyn, and their two little girls, Mia and Kianga, moved out there before we did. They were roomy houses but very dusty. There was little in the way of caulking around the windows. A dirt road was right in front, and every time a vehicle drove past, which was often, it would leave the kitchens with a layer of dirt. We managed to buy beds but little other furniture. There was an in-ground pool in the courtyard that we never filled. Another Bell family soon occupied the third villa. The Clacks' were from Philadelphia. They immediately got their swimming pool up and running, and their home became the gathering place. I did not want to be intrusive, so I spent most of my days in our home or at Scotty and Marilyn's. We finally got a refrigerator.

The stove would be next. Most mornings Dorjän and I ate a breakfast of cereal and flatbread with butter. Our other meals were often at Scotty and Marilyn's. I also had to do laundry at their place as well. This villa, however pleasant, never became a home.

Shortly after moving to Homayunshahr, I became pregnant. I was a bit frightened about whether or not I could get good prenatal care. I found an excellent doctor in the city. I was surprised at how up-to-date the equipment and practices of my doctor were. Still, we planned to have our second child in England and not in Esfahan.

During one of our excursions into Esfahan, someone broke into the villa and stole many of our belongings. We would never recover them. Now I no longer felt safe. I spent more time at Scotty and Marilyn's and visited the Clacks' once in a while. But he and Bobby did not have a good relationship, so I didn't go there often. Scotty and Marilyn were having difficulties. She was threatening to leave and go back to the States. She would become one of many wives who would leave the country and return home with their marriages in ruin.

So many ex-pat couples I met in Iran did not stay married. They were often isolated either by circumstances or by choice, one of the early warning signs. That isolation was a breeding ground for difficulties in their marriages. Drug and alcohol use, other attractions, and work gave these relationship destroyers too much room and freedom. The wives felt abandoned. Meeting people from all over the world was exciting, but many of these new relationships opened windows of opportunity for unfaithfulness. I don't think any of us were prepared for the physical and emotional isolation we encountered. Companies could do more to help employees manage working conditions that could destroy marriages and family relationships.

> *Secret: Isolation in your emotional or physical relationship slowly destroys trust and intimacy.*

Bobby:

After completing their orientation period, Scotty and his family rented a house in the city close to the girl's school. They lived there for a few weeks until Scotty connected with a group of Iranian Colonels seeking American families to rent the luxury villas they were building near the ancient village of Homayunshahr, a scenic drive 28 km from Esfahan. The deal was right, so they rented the first villa, and we moved into the one next door. An American family from Philadelphia took the third villa shortly after.

It was the perfect immersion, our own little Persian Paradise. The entrance was via a white marble foyer with an expansive gourmet kitchen off to the right, three bedrooms, two baths equipped with western and eastern facilities, and an enclosed courtyard with an in-ground swimming pool surrounded by fruit trees. We discovered just how complete the immersion was the first night we moved in. Needing milk and groceries, Scotty and I drove into the village to find a store. No one spoke any English. It was an hour before they found someone to translate. It seemed that the entire population had gathered to watch this amusing scene. I decided that night that I would become fluent in Farsi, the language of Iran.

Tricia:

One day Bobby was much later than usual coming home from work. We had no phone or way to contact one another. We often made our calls to the states from a public call center. When he did finally arrive home, he was distraught. He had hit an Iranian boy who had run in front of his car; then he took him to the hospital, which was an admission of guilt in Iranian law. Thankfully, the boy had only a broken leg. Bobby had to make restitution to the family, even though witnesses said the accident was the boy's fault and tried to convince him to leave the scene. He agreed to Bell paying the family and the medical expenses, deducting the reimbursement from his checks. It was not a huge amount, but for the family, it was significant. Nonetheless, it would cause us some financial hardship, especially since he was paid only once a month.

The Americans in Iran spent a great deal of time gathering with and without their families. Gatherings included liquor and other forms of stimulus such as marijuana and hashish. During this time, I noticed that Bobby was doing more recreational drugs. We had our spats about it. It was a daily routine for his brother and their friends to gather after work; get high; listen to music while eating large quantities of the pistachios indigenous to Iran. They talked about events in the States and the political shifts in Iran that were starting to prompt changes on the base.

Bobby was working his alternate job in the warehouse. He hated the confinement, especially after the daily excitement of aerial photography from helicopters. But I believe that God used this downtime for his spiritual conversion.

The Face-off

Tricia:

We were driving home late one night from visiting friends at the new housing complex. We found ourselves facing a tank staring down at us with armed soldiers waving guns and shouting. The nightly curfew had extended out to the villages. My husband has a gift of diplomacy and was educated about the culture of the people we lived among. These two things helped him secure our safe passage home and an apology from the officer in charge for frightening us. But we knew it was time to leave Homayunshahr, especially after Marilyn and the girls had left. I was home alone for increasingly more extended periods. We had to go out for meals, and I was simply tired of being isolated from other Americans. These changes made us realize we needed to be closer to the city.

Bobby:

Those were memorable times living in Homayunshahr, our season of seclusion. Unfortunately, it ended abruptly when martial law and the evening curfews extended beyond the city. One night we found ourselves in the middle of the highway facing head-on with an Army tank.

We spent a fun day hanging out with James Chambers and his wife from New York City, visiting other young black couples. They resided in Shāhīn Shahr, a newly built walled and gated compound, Iran's first master-planned satellite city, located approximately 24 km north of Esfahan. They were from all over the United States: Atlanta, GA; California, Chicago, IL; Texas, and Alabama. I love this culture of diversity. People come from all over the world to work in Iran.

As the ladies were getting acquainted, the guys were outside on the open field, engaged in an epic flag football game. Our only audience was an armed Iranian soldier dressed in an ill-fitting uniform standing in front of the gate where a helicopter manufacturing plant was under construction. He posed for my photograph after the game.

The rest of the evening was spent in lively conversation, enjoying the potluck dinner and playing cards. At the same time, English-speaking television played muted in the background, an ethnic tradition in that era. When the political disputes between Cleveland mayor Dennis Kucinich and city council president George Forbes came on the screen, someone noticed and turned the volume up. Of all the events happening in the world at that time, they broadcasted our hometown's mess.

Night had fallen by the time we loaded up the Fiat to head home. The drive was pleasant and uneventful until suddenly, coming directly towards us were blinding headlights. I began flashing my high beams to signal them to get over. It became evident that the vehicle in question was stationary, just sitting in the middle of the road. In front of the tank were soldiers kneeling and aiming their guns at us. I stopped the car. The officer in charge approached the vehicle and gruffly asked why we were out after the curfew? I greeted him cordially (as was the custom) in Farsi. He quickly apologized for his rudeness. I explained that we did not realize the curfew was being enforced this far from the city. He expressed total surprise, even disbelief, that Americans lived out here in the villages so far from the western communities. They escorted us home and watched until we unlocked our front door (making sure we lived there) and went inside.

This encounter made us realize that living in this rural location had become too volatile and isolated during the present political climate. Our season of total immersion had come to an end. We would move again for the fifth time.

CHAPTER 10
Move #5: *Toy Furniture*

Tricia:

We did not find housing right away. We stayed with Herbert and Vanessa Fletcher, a family from San Francisco, California, who we met at the Suite Hotel. Their daughter Dyanne was about Dorjän's age. I was thankful he had a playmate.

We moved our footlockers and bed into their small place. Our room was barely large enough for the bed. I was having morning sickness, and the crowded arrangements were not ideal. They had only a tiny bathroom that I remember spending a lot of time in. Still, I was grateful that we were there. Vanessa and I took turns cooking. When you have to plan meals, shop every day and cook mostly everything from scratch, meal preparation can consume a lot of time. I also enjoyed the courtyard and the figs that grew there. It was modest in size but a good place for Dorjän and Dyanne to play.

Bobby:

We met Herbert and Vanessa and their adorable daughter Dyanne the first day they checked into the Suite Hotel. They were a tall, attractive couple from San Francisco. We hit it off immediately and began spending a lot of time together. They had found a quaint but small place in the city and invited us to stay with them until we found new housing. Herbert and I would sit up at night after everyone went to bed talking and smoking weed (marijuana). We would squeeze ourselves into a couple of wrought iron chairs from Dyanne's tea set, enjoying great conversations and trying not to wake up the house.

I was impressed with his excitement and genuine enthusiasm from recently finding Christ in his life. I was firmly set in my agnosticism but found the intimacy and ease of his relationship with his faith disarming. He never tried to persuade me; instead, he was just living out his personal experience.

My fondest memory of Herbert was that night while sitting in those tiny wrought iron chairs talking about the Iranian soldiers on the base taunting us and trying to get us into trouble. Herbert hunched his broad shoulders and said, "Oh, don't hurt 'em, Holy Ghost!"

CHAPTER 11
Move #6: *Back To City Life*

Tricia:

We finally found a second-floor apartment in the Mahale Now Khajoo Koocheh in the French Quarter close to downtown Esfahan. The landlord and his family lived on the ground floor of the duplex. It was a lovely place, partly furnished, including a stove, refrigerator, and washing machine, which was great because we had less cash since Bobby's paycheck deductions from the car accident.

The neighbors would garden, hang laundry and walk around on their rooftop patios. As the turmoil in the city started to rise, we would stand on our rooftop and plan escape routes. Sometimes the demonstrators would gather on the corner and march down the street. As they walked past, I could hear the chants outside my kitchen window of "Allah Akbar" and "Americans go home."

Nonetheless, I did not wish to go home. I had grown to love the country and the people of Iran. The only real news about what was happening came through the American Companies. It was more in daily releases expressing protocols Americans should take when out and about. But at the time, it didn't seem too alarming. I enjoyed walking about, shopping, and even meeting new friends who lived within walking distance. I had friends we could visit who didn't live far from us. We enjoyed a lovely Thanksgiving meal with them, other Americans, and a couple from apartheid South Africa. The conversations mostly centered around the growing intensity of living in Iran. I began wondering about our safety and worrying whether I should go back home soon. I knew I would not be able to fly after my seventh month of pregnancy.

Bobby:

We moved into a modern second-floor apartment in a quaint little neighborhood across from downtown Esfahan. The landlord and his family were friendly people. They apparently supported the Shah's view of modern Iran, judging by their European dress style. Prudence dictated that we live above ground level with all the ensuing political unrest.

We witnessed at least two street demonstrations (while peeking through the window) march right below our apartment. One night I even tiptoed on the rooftops to mark out an escape route for us should that become necessary. When our landlord thought it politically advantageous to side with the Khomeini factions, it became inconvenient to have Americans staying on his property. He was breaking the lease and requiring us to move out almost immediately. After realizing there was no altering his decision, I said a very insulting and derogatory phrase to him in perfect Farsi (which I regret doing). I didn't know the exact English translation, but the Iranian soldier who taught me said it would make him angry enough to want to kill me. We would move for the seventh time.

Ducks All Lined Up — Then Came Jesus
Islamic Republic of Iran Army Aviation (IRIAA) Helicopter Base - Sunday, 5 November 1978

Bobby:

My contract with Bell required working dual positions. My primary position was Special Programs Photographer. The other assignment was working in the hangar on the base doing the mundane job of monitoring the Spectrometric Oil Analysis Program for the helicopter line. A far cry from the exciting photography assignments I enjoyed most days, especially when I had the opportunity to fly.

As usual, it took about an hour to collect and complete the analysis of the oil samples. That concluded my work for the day. I settled in for the long hours before my shift ended. On this particular day, after writing a couple of letters home to friends and family, I began considering what I had accomplished since arriving in Iran. I wanted to achieve a certain level of perfection in my life. That was the goal.

I thought that I had "All my ducks lined up all in a row," as the saying goes. My marriage, family, dream job, good income, growing social circle, custom gold jewelry, handmade Persian rugs, enjoying exquisite strains of cannabis, hashish, fine food, and drink. But still, I wasn't fulfilled; it felt like I had a void, a big hole in my soul.

Then a voice, more like an impression, spoke to me, saying, "Only I can fill that hole; it's just for me." I don't remember if I said it out loud or just to myself, but I said,

"Well, fill it then!" It felt like a touch in the middle of my forehead that permeated the depths of my soul. I knew that it would be with me forever. It was as if the "wind was blowing" and the soul of a prophet had passed through me. Those were the only words I could think of to describe what I was experiencing. Everything felt different, new, and peaceful. I began writing my thoughts into the little Standard Memo Book that I always kept with me (which I still have to this day). I did not fully understand what had just happened to me, but I left that hangar a new man that day, somehow knowing that this feeling, this transformation, would last for the rest of my life.

Tricia:

I trusted Christ for my salvation at about twelve years of age. I was influenced by some books in our home with colorful pictures depicting God and creation and the stories of Moses and Noah. These images and stories fascinated me. I wondered about this God who loved these people in the stories so much. I knew I wanted that same God to love me as well. Early on, I read Old Testament stories and the New Testament Gospels. It wasn't until I attended a neighborhood Bible study that I was introduced to Christ. I was instantly changed when I said "Yes" to Jesus as my Lord and Savior. Of course, I didn't really know much about what that meant because my family did not go to church. I always knew, even without being discipled, that God was with me. I continued to explore other faiths out of curiosity, but my heart belonged to Jesus.

When I met Bobby and married, I knew nothing about being "unequally yoked" or what that meant. But I did know that worldly influences governed our lives.

So on that day in Iran, when Bobby walked into our kitchen with a glow that I had never seen before, the Holy Spirit immediately let me know what had happened to him. I believe it was because God's Spirit was now in him, agreeing with His Spirit in me. I asked him, "What happened to you today?" He told me of his conversion experience. I was so grateful to God that we were now united in faith. God's guidance would get us through some tough days that would soon be ahead of us. This same unity of faith would preserve our marriage in the distant future.

> ***Secret:*** *Being vertically aligned spiritually and connected horizontally makes for a powerful and enduring relationship.*

CHAPTER 12
Move #7: Returning To Western Society

Tricia:

We decided, for now, that it would be prudent to live in one of the condominium communities, so we applied for housing at Shāhīn Shahr, the newest housing complex that American companies provide for their employees. Iranian critics referred to them as American ghettos. We thought it would be safer to live with other Americans under the present circumstances. There was a long waiting list, so we could not move right away. We kept our foot-lockers packed in case we needed to move quickly.

We moved in with James, our friend from New York City. James lived in the Khan-A Isfahan complex with his girlfriend and their baby. He and his wife broke up, and she returned home. It was close to Christmas, things were escalating, and we needed to get our stuff from our apartment. We planned to stay with James only until we could get our new housing.

The volatility of the situation was evident when Bobby went back to the Mahale Now apartment to get the rest of our things. The landlord padlocked the door after his neighbors found out that Americans lived in his place. Black people living in Iran were often mistaken for Palestinian or African instead of American. Our landlord had told the protestors that we were African. When it became apparent that we were American, an angry crowd gathered in front of the house. Using his ability to de-escalate tense situations, Bobby got the remainder of our belongings and left without incident.

Living at James' place made me feel a little safer; they had armed guards at the gate. We stayed indoors mostly unless we had to walk to the store. The walk was a good three to four miles round trip. It was a military commissary, so getting more food and brands I was accustomed to from the States was nice. I did not have to cook often; James enjoyed cooking and was good at it. I didn't want to inconvenience him or his girlfriend, so I tried to give them their space. I stayed in our room a lot, hoping that we would have our own place by Christmas. Since April, we have been in Iran, but I never felt settled in.

Aside from baking a cake, we spent most of Christmas Day in our room. I drew a Christmas tree on a white poster board, topped with a handmade aluminum foil star, that we taped on the wall. Dorjän had a good Christmas. He loved the few items we found for him and spent the day playing as any child would.

I found a secretary job with the Northrop Grumman Corporation and would begin working after Christmas. I was excited about making extra money, and Dorjän would be in a preschool near me. Unfortunately, I never got the chance to start.

The situation was getting tense. Reports of Iranians sending their families to the United States and Americans sending their families home were daily news. We were beginning to wonder if we would be staying as well. James sent his family home. We did not want to burden him anymore, so we moved again. Every day, Bell would put out an update on possible evacuation procedures and advise everyone in the meantime "to keep a low profile." Still, many of us hoped and felt that things would return to normal.

Bobby:

This situation was becoming more volatile by the day. Either Bell would be sending us home, or this conflict would pass, and business as usual would resume. The U.S. Government's prediction leaned toward the latter, hoping all of this would blow over. Tricia had gotten hired as a secretary for Northrop Corporation and would begin working after the Christmas break. We planned to bank her entire paycheck and start aggressively saving and investing for our future.

Martial law was declared in August following the reporting of a series of violent events. The volatility of this rapidly approaching revolution precipitated the early departure of many Bell employees and their families. Leaving without the prerequisite evacuation orders was a breach of contract. It would unofficially blackball them from obtaining other lucrative international assignments. Some opted to stay and wait while their spouses and children left without them. Many families fell apart from the pressure, including my brother Scotty's family. They soon divorced after his family left Iran.

Tricia and I decided to stay together, especially since she was five months pregnant, and we had the blessing of hospitality extended to us by our friends. We had come full circle in our living arrangements. Before these events, we enjoyed the incredible experience of living immersed in Homayunshahr. Unfortunately, living in such isolation was no longer a safe option. The Iranian people were approaching a cataclysmic revolution that would cause upheaval in their lives for years to come.

We did not want to sign another lease in the interim of moving to our new housing at Shāhīn Shahr. We spent the Christmas holidays in James' spare bedroom, then Ray Davis invited us to move in with him until his wife and daughter arrived in the new year. Both James and Ray lived in Khan-A Isfahan.

CHAPTER 13
Move #8: *Strikes, Tragedy, and Transitions*

Tricia:

We soon found ourselves living with Ray Davis when the power workers went on strike. They would turn off the electricity each night from about 8:00 to 11:00 PM. Because of Ray's high-level tech job, Bell assigned an armed Iranian guard on his roof. I learned to play backgammon, and we spent hours playing cards, telling stories, and discussing escape plans. Somehow though, we kept thinking things would not get much worse.

One evening Ray got a dreadful phone call. His wife and daughter had been killed in a car accident in Los Angeles, CA. He would have to return home immediately. He was still hoping his family would join him in Iran as scheduled until that call. I was glad we were there for him. He graciously invited us to remain in his place while he was gone. Bobby felt it would be good to accompany him on the drive to Tehran to get his flight. It would be the last time we would see Ray.

Now, it seemed that it was inevitable we would be returning to the U.S, or at least leaving Iran. Demonstrations were more frequent in the city. Bobby's drive to and from work became tedious because of the protests. American women could not go outdoors without having their heads covered. We tried to sell as many things as possible while waiting to leave. The last item to sell was the Fiat. It had become increasingly dangerous to live in the city. Hence, our friend Pachaco Dorello moved in with us at Ray's condo.

Bobby:

We didn't know it at the time, but moving in with Ray would be our last move in-country. Ray was a Weapons Systems Specialist for Bell. Former LAPD (Los Angeles Police Department), a licensed cosmetologist, and a martial artist. Ray was sharp. We met one night at the club and connected as martial arts practitioners.

The government worker's strike in Esfahan had begun. They would turn off the electricity every evening from around 8:00 to 11:00 PM. We made it our dinner and relaxing time to make the best of this inconvenience. Ray called it "chillaxing." Tricia and Ray prepared the food before the lights went out. We would dine by candlelight, then drink wine and cognac while listening to jazz on Ray's battery-powered radio.

Soon after moving in, Ray had to return home to California due to the tragic car accident that took his wife and child. My heart still aches for his loss. I accompanied him on the taxi ride to Tehran to catch his flight to Los Angeles, a ride engulfed in silence. One can only imagine the shock, grief, and powerlessness Ray was suffering. An incident triggered the rawness of his emotions which I believe exposed the true purpose of my presence on this trip.

Grief and the Immortal

Along with the enactment of Martial Law, curfews, and strikes, gasoline shortages caused long lines at the stations. Midway to Tehran, we stopped to refuel. We sat in awkward silence for about 30 minutes until an Iranian man walking past our taxi noticed that two foreigners were in the back seat and began to pound his fist on the hood while shouting to the crowd. The noise yanked Ray out of his silent reverie and ignited his rage. Disregarding the prevailing situation, being the only Americans there, he reached for the door handle to get out of the car and engage the source of his irritation. Our "keeping a low profile" posture was about to change without any prospects of favorable results. I had already noticed that one of the Shah's war-hardened "Immortals" (an elite military unit) stood guard at the gas station entrance. I shuddered when I looked into that soldier's eyes; all I saw was death. I grabbed Ray's arm, pulled him close to me, and said, "I'm with you, man! I'll take the hundred on my right, and you take the hundred on your left!"

That did the trick; he broke into laughter, and we eased back into our seats and talked about his wife and daughter, beginning the healing process through the stages of his grief. I was so relieved that he did not open that car door! The rest of the trip was uneventful. Thank God!

Ray and I discussed our mutual friend Pacheco's housing situation during the ride. He had to move from his apartment in the volatile Armenian section. It was no longer safe for any foreigner to live in the city. Ray consented to Pacheco moving into his condo with us in his absence. That's the kind of guy Ray was; a giver. Even in his grief, he was thinking of others.

After our farewells, I stayed the night with my brother Scotty, who had transferred to the base in Tehran. I was hoping to visit the renowned ski resort while there, but it rained that evening, so I headed back to Esfahan the following day.

I would not see or hear from Ray Davis again.

The Honeymoon Is Over — It's Time To Go Home
Friday, 26 January 1979 - 4:00 PM IRST

Ray wasn't the only one who left the country abruptly. Many Europeans and Americans left Iran during these turbulent times. Bell distributed daily bulletins detailing the incidents of violence throughout the city the previous day, many involving Americans. Mobs of people gathered daily, marching, protesting, adamantly declaring which side they were supporting; the Shah or the Ayatollah. Cars overturned and set on fire were a nightly occurrence, as were the attacks and beating of foreigners. We did our best to avoid the demonstrations. Still, several times while driving in the city, a mob of demonstrators would come upon us seemingly out of nowhere. We had to quickly determine which faction they supported and either put a picture of the Shah or Khomeini in the car window as we drove through. Choosing the wrong photo would be disastrous. The crowd would attack the vehicles, even turning some of them over. Fortunately, we always chose correctly.

Counting Down
Monday, 29 January 1979 - 8:00 AM IRST

Bell had finally issued the official evacuation orders for their employees to leave Iran. I had mixed emotions about leaving, especially two years earlier than expected. We were not ready to go; we were just getting our feet under us; Iran was starting to feel like home.

All evacuees had to report to the Hotel Kourosh in downtown Esfahan by 5:00 PM Monday to turn in equipment and process final paperwork. Bell hired a fleet of buses to take us to Tehran for our evacuation flights departing on Wednesday. Just 12 hours before Ayatollah Khomeini's scheduled arrival in Tehran from Paris, France.

Tricia and Dorjän would spend the day packing our nine-foot-lockers for the company to ship back to the states. Pacheco and I got an early start. We had a few items to sell but did not have the benefit days or weeks required for the proper tarof. Nonetheless, it was a festive, fast-paced, and productive day. We made a good team. He and I both enjoyed the city's energy and the cadence of the Tarof. We sold every item that could not be shipped or carried out of the country. Pacheco had large appliances and furniture, and I had my memorable red Fiat 128 SL and other small items.

After I sold the car, we hailed a taxi. The driver and his friend were interested in buying Pacheco's last item. We sat relaxed in the back seat, taking our final drive through the city while listening to them discuss their bargaining strategy. With the recent departure of Iran's Royal Family, everyone knew that the foreigners would not be far behind. They intended to use our urgency to broker an unreasonably low price as a bargaining strategy. Of course, they had no idea that we could speak and understand our fair share of

Farsi. Visibly embarrassed when we finished the negotiations using their language, we leveraged this loss of face into an excellent deal.

We arrived at the Hotel Kourosh around 4:00, an hour before the cutoff.

The S*** Hits The Fan
Monday, 29 January 1979 – 4:15 PM IRST

I left Pacheco to pay the cab fare and ran up the winding staircase to the second-floor conference room. It was not that crowded, so I began processing my paperwork. Almost finished, I started to wonder, what was taking him so long? Suddenly, a commotion at the door demanded everyone's attention. Pacheco burst into the room, rushing up to me with a wild, panicked look in his eyes. Shoving his flight jacket into my arms, he told me there was an incident, and he ended up shooting the taxi driver in the face. He had wrapped the gun in his flight jacket; most of us carried a concealed weapon for protection during these last few weeks of unrest.

I would not find out until years later about the dispute between Pacheco and the taxi driver over a previously unsettled fare. After I left the taxi, their disagreement turned into an argument that quickly escalated to the precipice of violence. A crowd of locals gathered, suddenly surrounding Pacheco and the taxi driver. Pacheco felt isolated and trapped as the mob became aggressive and advanced. Fearing for his safety and possibly his life, he took off, running toward the park across the street. While being chased, something clicked in his mind; "Enough of this; I'm not running any further." He pulled out the small pistol concealed in the interior pocket of his flight jacket; slightly turning, barely aiming, he fired, hitting the taxi driver in the face, then ran into the hotel.

It didn't take long for Bell's Chief of Security to assess the situation. He quickly moved everyone across the hall to a more secure room. While they barricaded the door, I dropped Pacheco's gun on the thickly carpeted floor. Then kicked it under the long drapes covering the rear window. I would eventually have to give it to the officials but kept the #119 Buck Hunting Knife I got from Ray Davis hidden in the small of my back. I still have it to this day.

A Daring Escape

With all the focus on Pacheco's situation, no one noticed the American jumping out of the rear window. His name was Whitey Lockman, a Caucasian man from Texas. He and I had some history; he was the only person who called me a racial slur the entire time I was in Iran. This happened during my first week in Esfahan in the lobby of the Suite Hotel. I was young, radical, and hotheaded. If my brother Scotty had not held me back, I would have physically assaulted that man, no doubt resulting in Bell immediately sending me home. A few months later, I ran into Whitey on the street. He apologized for his earlier behavior toward me and offered me a ride. His wife and family left him and went back to the states. We sat in his car, talking and sharing a sip of vodka from his flask. Life does indeed have a tendency to come full circle.

A Life Held In Balance

The international press reported over 5,000 people demonstrated in the streets outside the hotel. Martial law has been in full force for almost four months. This revolution was rapidly approaching its crescendo. The scheduled arrival of Ayatollah Sayyid Ruhollah Musavi Khomeini, the Islamic Republic leader, was just two days away. The Shah of Iran, Mohammad Reza Pahlavi, and his family fled a few weeks ago, triggering more frequent and blatant attacks on British and U.S. expatriates, whom the Iranians regard as symbols of Westernization.

After hours of intense negotiations by Bell Helicopter officials, U.S. Consul David McGaffey, and the all black-clad Mullahs (local Islamic clerics), Pacheco was remanded into the custody of the Iranian authorities.

To celebrate his last day in Iran, Pacheco wore some of his unique and expensive jewelry. Before they took him away, he gave it all to me, requesting that I get it to his father in New York City. I especially remember that exquisite jade and gold necklace handcrafted by his brother-in-law, a Buddhist monk in Thailand. The black-clad Mullahs then led Pacheco out of the room. I only saw the back of his head and the sleeves of his flight jacket with handcuffed hands held high.

I would mail his package when I got home, but I wondered if I would ever see him again.

What's Next?
Tuesday, 30 January 1979 – 3:00 AM IRST

This hostage event was finally over. We waited inside the hotel for *over* an hour until the crowd dispersed. It's now 3:00 in the morning; I've been out of contact with Tricia since we left early yesterday; she must be crazy worried.

An eerie light fog blanketed the parking lot, providing a welcomed peace, muffling the sounds of protest, unrest, and turbulence of the past few hours. A few Iranian men and boys were milling around the parking lot—stragglers whose adrenaline was still pumping from the previous days' events. No doubt restless and apprehensive, anticipating the transition of power their country was about to enter.

I don't remember who loaned me the keys to their car, just that it wouldn't start. Esfahanians are always eager to help with a stalled vehicle or one that slipped off the road while navigating the narrow alleyways throughout the city. They headed towards me in the parking lot. Experiencing panic at being alone, isolated, and recognized as a foreigner, I waved them off as they approached the car. The ignition finally caught. As the small engine came to life, I quickly drove off as they were running after me, yelling, "American, American!"

These past few days have been a blur, packed with many events. Being married for only 303 days, we are still practically newlyweds. We never imagined being caught up in a revolution halfway around the world from home. Even so, our short stay in this ancient mystical country would change our lives forever.

Tricia:

The evening before our evacuation was long and frightening. Bobby and Pacheco left early in the day to sell the car and Pacheco's appliances before completing the evacuation process at a hotel in town. I did not hear from him for hours. I was in a state of panic. Bobby finally returned home in the middle of the night, alone. He filled me in on what happened and why he was delayed.

CHAPTER 14
Move #9: *Evacuation*

Tricia:

A car was supposed to pick us up and take us to the hotel to board a bus to Tehran. My second wave of panic came when the car never showed up; I was afraid we would miss the bus. It was clear that Americans needed to be out of Iran as soon as possible. Bobby drove us to the hotel in the car he had borrowed to get home. We grabbed the luggage we would carry and left. The footlockers were packed, locked, and labeled, ready to be transported to the airport and flown back to the states. They never made it out of Iran.

Only a few people were at the hotel when we pulled up. There should have been hundreds, and only one bus was left from the fleet of 13. Because of the incident the day before, they had no intention of letting Bobby go just yet. They wanted to detain and question him further. He convinced them he knew nothing more about the shooting incident, and they could not keep him any longer. Here I was with my young son, pregnant and frightened by the fact that we might be left in a country that no longer wanted us there. The three of us boarded that bus to Tehran. After a very intense conversation between Bobby and the driver, we were finally on our way.

The trip to Tehran was frightening, especially since the driver stopped to pick up people along the way, even though he was hired to transport only Bell employees and their families. Bobby slept from exhaustion. I sat up with Dorjän, praying we would not be stopped by a mob or put off the bus in the middle of the road. Arriving in Tehran, the driver got so nervous when the traffic came to a complete stop; he put us off the bus blocks from the hotel; we walked the rest of the way. I was just glad we made it to Tehran safely. Our flight would leave the following day, and I was absolutely ready to go home.

On the other hand, Bobby was not ready to go back to the states. He felt he had to return because of my pregnancy, so we could not take the option of going to another country with Bell or any other company. We returned to the states and moved in with his parents. Everything we owned was in our suitcases and Bobby's camera bag. Our nine-footlockers never made it home. We have been married for just ten months. We were starting over financially, spiritually, and soon to have another baby.

> *"Life takes you to unexpected places. Love brings you home." - Melissa McClone*

Every challenge and obstacle we faced was a proving ground for our relationship and our marriage. I learned a lot about myself in those ten months; as a person, a wife, a mother, a Christian, and an American. But the one thing that I truly believed made the difference in how we met each situation and what sustained us was our faith in God.

Iran was more than a country where we lived for a few months; it became the birthplace of Bobby's relationship with Christ. Iran will forever be endeared in our hearts and minds. It was here that our mettle was tested as individuals and as a newly married couple.

Bobby:

If someone had told us 300 days ago (our wedding day) that we would end up in the middle of a revolution, I would have thought them crazy. So many things happened so rapidly: We have moved nine times in as many months.

Even our evacuation was complicated. I had to practically hijack the last bus out of the fleet of 13 that Bell provided to transport the evacuees to Tehran for the outgoing flights. The other buses had left by the time we arrived. The authorities wanted to determine my involvement in Pacheco shooting the taxi driver, so they gave me the incorrect departure time. However, since eyewitnesses verified that I was already inside the hotel at the time, they had no grounds to detain me further.

The next hurdle was getting the bus driver to take us to Tehran. Everyone else had already left, and this bus was the extra one in case of overflow. He did not want to go. The cordial Tarof quickly escalated to threats and demands that he take us because he was already paid. The visual of my wife holding her five months pregnant stomach while cuddling our three-year-old son didn't hurt. The three of us were the only passengers on this comfortable Mercedes-Benz touring bus. Exhausted, I slept all the way there. The traffic came to a standstill a few blocks from the destination hotel. Our driver got very nervous having Americans on board, so he pulled over, insisting we exit the bus right there. There was no persuading him to go further, so we walked the remaining block or so with our luggage.

My brother Scotty met us at the hotel and was very surprised to see us. When we didn't arrive earlier with the first group of evacuees from Esfahan, he found out that the CIA wanted me detained for their investigation into the previous day's events. What I didn't know at the time was that Pacheco and the U.S. Consul David McGaffey were beaten by the crowd outside the hotel after Pacheco's arrest. No wonder those guys came after me in the parking lot. It's definitely time to go!

CHAPTER 15
Boomerang: *Back to "The World"*
تهران *Tehran, Iran – Wednesday, 31 January 1979*

Bobby:

My contract with Bell was for three years, but this revolution forced us to leave before completing year one. I was devastated that our plans were being obliterated right before our eyes. Tricia and I pulled up all roots to make this journey, selling or giving away anything that wouldn't fit into our suitcases or nine-foot-lockers. I even parted with my cherished Trans Am! I was determined and confident that I would make my mark as an international professional and lay the foundation for a secure financial future. We had no plans to move back to Ohio, none! We considered Fort Worth, TX, an attractive destination after our contract in Iran. The city was beginning a growth boom and was close to Bell's headquarters in Bedford. I was hoping to stay on as a staff photographer. Now everything has changed.

The following morning our entire group was on the tarmac looking up at the gigantic C-141 MAC (Military Airlift Command) cargo plane that would be our ride out. We expected a regular commercial flight, but we had no complaints, especially with the Ayatollah landing in a few hours; get us out of here! Athens was only a 3 ½ hour's flight, but it seemed worlds away. I was concerned about Tricia riding on those cots in her condition and very apprehensive about the mystery items they loaded on the plane behind the green tarp. Thankfully, the flight was without incident.

Athens
Wednesday, 31 January 1979

After checking into our hotel, we hit the streets to look around and find some food. Greece was a welcome change from the pressures of our last days in Iran. We dined that evening at a quaint little Greek restaurant, then got a restful night's sleep before heading home to the states the next day. We had an open ticket, and many of our single friends stayed in Athens to look for work, moving into youth hostels after the paid hotel time ended. I was envious of them. I wanted to stay in Greece, find employment and continue our adventure, but we had to return to the states due to Tricia's pregnancy. She was right that flying would be dangerous for her and the baby. I would not realize the level of regret that festered in me until years later, manifesting itself in very negative ways.

Coffee Conversation
South Euclid, OH - Kitchen Table - July 2015 10 AM EDT

B: The reality is that we ended up going through the beginning of the Iranian revolution. Some couples broke up from just that stress alone.

T: Yeah, we got through it, but there were a lot of challenges in those nine months, especially for a newly married couple.

B: Yep, and then coming back to the states unexpectedly.

T: Yep

B: We witnessed several relationships destroyed from the pressures of living over there

T: And some of it was from their own mess that didn't have anything to do with what was going on in the country

B: What do you mean?

T: I think, for the most part, a lot of it had to do with the stuff people were doing

B: What do you mean?

T: I saw people's relationships in trouble because the spouses were out whoring around, drinking and drugging, and doing everything else. You know families were in isolation; I was isolated

B: Yeah?

T: You didn't see, you didn't feel it; I had a whole different experience of Iran than you did

B: Okay?

T: You were very active with people every day; you were out. I was in the house with just me and Jacy, isolated

B: Especially in Homyaunshah

T: *All day long, especially out there, I was very isolated, and then when Marilyn left, I was really isolated*

B: *I didn't think about that*

T: *So I was like, you know..., this isolation is not good*

B: *Was it like that when we stayed in the city?*

T: *In Esfahan it was different. I could get out, go shopping, whatever; I wasn't tied to the house.*

B: *Right*

T: *Out there, I was tied to the house, couldn't do anything, and then Clack's wife was there, but I didn't really know her., I went around there a few times, but because you and Clack's relationship was so...*

B: *Volatile, he got on my last nerve*

T: *Yeah, so I didn't have a relationship with her. I didn't go around there as much as I would have because of your relationship with him.*

B: *You needed a car out there*

T: *I was very isolated, okay, so that led me to the point where we were going to move, or I was going home. And then you had your issues too with what you were doing, but, you know, so that was it*

B: *What issues do you mean, getting high?*

T: *Yeah! That was a big part of it. Every day! That was what your world centered around at that point, you being around those guys and getting high. I'm like, really - I did not come all this way for that.*

B: *Hmm*

T: *Okay!*

B: *Hmm, you know what ... the weird thing about that... I'm sorry; I apologize again*

T: *(chuckling) Yeah, okay*

PART III
THE COFFEEHOUSE CONVERSATIONS

Since the 17th century, when coffeehouses appeared outside the Ottoman Empire in Europe, they have continued to (arguably) be the best venue for conversation, "spreading enlightenment, intellectualism, and culture across multiple empires and continents."

This is a fact that remains true, even today.

CHAPTER 16
Don't Just Eavesdrop, Join Us!
Arabica Coffee House- Shaker Square Cleveland, OH - 1 January 1987

We love this coffeehouse, perfectly nestled between quaint little boutiques, an open-air market, and locally owned and operated restaurants. Everyone hung out here, but still, we didn't expect it to be this crowded on a chilly 38° New Year's Day. The atmosphere was bustling with the excitement of new beginnings and the residual effects from last night's end-of-year celebrations. Spotting an empty table across the room, we hurried over with our coffee and pastries in hand before it was gone. The ever-present music, coupled with the high vaulted ceilings and thick wood-paneled walls, created an invisible sound partition between the closely positioned tables, the ideal acoustics for engaging in private conversation.

We had been reminiscing about the long night before our evacuation from Iran. It was during our first year of marriage. I was detained for hours as one of the hostages during the negotiations after my friend Pacheco shot a taxi driver. We typically don't pay much attention to the people around us when we're talking; after all, isn't that one of the attractions of the coffeehouse phenomenon? I noticed movement from the table next to us out of my periphery. The people were leaning towards us, eavesdropping. What was so intriguing? I remember thinking, "Don't just eavesdrop; join us!." I said to Tricia, "wouldn't it be interesting if we could invite people into our conversations? We could talk about our life and the lessons we've learned that make our relationship successful."

That was the moment of inspiration; the assignment for this book came to me. "God, you mean this for Tricia, right, not for me; she's the writer?" Like Moses, I felt inadequate for this task. The Bible says that Moses deferred his call from God to his brother Aaron because he thought he could not speak well. Tricia has always been an excellent writer, excelling in her collegiate studies in journalism. I'm just a hacker in comparison. He responded, "if she writes it, that's her gift; if you write it, I get the glory because you can't write!" God indeed has a sense of humor.

"Whole Bean the Marriage Blend" was conceived. Our initial idea was to create a coffee table booklet, a memoir primarily for our children. We thought it would be beneficial if our parents had provided a journal or ledger of their experiences. How did they keep it together for so long?

A few years would pass before we began recording our conversations. At the various coffee shops throughout the city, over copious cups of coffee, we discussed the events of our lives. What we agree upon, as well as our conflicting views and opinions. What was working for us, and most importantly, what was not. No subject was off the table.

While transcribing these discussions, we discovered a few principles that kept our relationship healthy, happy, successful and thriving, not just suffering and surviving. That's no way to live, regardless of how long a couple has been together.

> ***Secret:*** *The foundational moments that relationships are constructed upon are critical components to their success. Pay close attention to the blueprint you're developing.*

CHAPTER 17
My Daddy's Cup
Caribou Coffee - Coventry Village Cleveland Heights, OH - June 2003

This lovely coffee shop is just below street level in Coventry Village. An eclectic, easily walkable neighborhood, home to many independently-owned businesses. We loved enjoying our coffee sitting on the counter-height bar stools in front of the large street-level windows while watching the unique diversity of people stroll past. The slogans printed on their napkins; "Life is Short, Stay Awake for it" or "Life is too short to Drink Bad Coffee," capture the energy of this area.

I take my coffee black — no cream — no sugar. When asked why just black, my answer is always that my wife is cream & sugar enough for me.

Tricia orders her coffee with cream and sugar. Here we go, again.

B: Why do you mess up an excellent cup of gourmet coffee with cream and sugar? You should at least taste it before adding anything to it.

T: I can taste this coffee just fine, and I enjoy it with cream and sugar.

We go round and round with this issue. The initial plan was to spend some pleasurable time together people-watching while drinking our coffee. Perhaps some stimulating conversation which usually is a prelude to a romantic evening.

B: Why do you insist on drinking your coffee that way?
T: Because this is how I like it.
B: Why do you like it that way?

We've made it to our window seats by now, drinking our coffee while having this animated debate. The people walking past the window watched us instead of us watching them. Tricia pauses, reflects, leans closer, and says...

T: When I was a little girl, I drank coffee from my Daddy's cup. He would always add extra cream and sugar just for me so it wouldn't be so strong. Daddy was an Executive Chef. I would often accompany him when he catered to private events and worked at various country clubs. Every time I drink my coffee this way, I relive some of the special times spent with him while growing up.

I admit to being somewhat of a coffee aficionado. I've been drinking my coffee black for a few years now. We have been having debates about this issue ever since. Until that moment, we had not peeled away enough layers to get to the bottom of it. The treasure of discovering something rooted in my wife's persona was fascinating. This exhibits a commitment to the relationship. The principles of persistence, patience, respect, and perspective are what we're dealing with here.

CHAPTER 18
Men & Shopping
University Heights, OH – Starbucks Cedar Center – circa 2003

I was one of the few men on the walking tour of the private homes in Rockefeller's Forest Hill Historic District. We enjoyed a wonderful afternoon touring those unique homes and meeting the owners. Afterward, I found myself shopping with Tricia at the Kaufman's on the Heights department store for a pair of black slacks. I showed her one that I thought she would like almost as soon as we entered the store. She, of course, proceeded to shop the entire section, eventually going back to purchase the one I picked out in the beginning.

At the checkout counter, an older woman in the line asked Tricia, "How did you get your husband to go shopping with you? My husband never goes with me." Then two other women chimed in with their comments. I shop with my wife all the time, so what was the big deal? We left the store and picked up the discussion at the Starbucks cafe across the street.

T: So, did you enjoy it?

B: Actually, I enjoy shopping with you but only on my terms.

T: What do you mean by that?

B: Well, you have to understand that we men are essentially hunter-gatherers. I love spending time shopping with you, especially when you model for me.

T: You need to finish that thought.

B: Which thought?

T: The hunter-gather thing" (I noticed how she picked only one of the two points I put out there)

B: Well, you see, men need to have an explicit purpose for shopping. If we get hungry, we go to the grocery store; run out of underwear - the department store. So if you express a need for a pair of black pants or a dress for my cousin's birthday dinner cruise, my response is to go hunting for it.

T: Ok, that's one point. But when men shop with their wives, they desire to hunt, find that one item and get out. You immediately found a pair of black Capri in my size upon entering the store, but you still didn't rush me.

B: When I shop with you, I carve out time to enjoy the experience at your pace. My experience is that rushing you usually ends badly. Then you begin to bring up all the related incidents of bad times from the past. So I've learned to exercise patience when shopping with you. When you shop with me, it's on! I tell you what I'm looking for, and when I find it, I get it. Right?

T: Yep, that's what you do. So you enjoy shopping with me because you've learned how to make the experience pleasurable for you, right?

B: *Whatever you say.*

T: *I have to confess that I've taken it for granted. It wasn't until those ladies made those comments that I appreciated it.*

B: *It's like a well-practiced golf swing. It's supposed to look effortless.*

T: *Well, the fact that you usually pay for my purchases doesn't hurt either. So how does a woman get her man to shop with her and have a good time?*

B: *Basically, all men love to shop. We love shopping for what we want or need at that time. We will spend hours, days, and even months hunting for that vintage sports car or the latest power tool—the motivation being to get what we want when we want it. So women could suggest (to their husbands) that they would get sex out of the deal. (winking) Plus, you have to make the shopping experience pleasurable and fun. I enjoy it when you give me a private show by modeling your prospective purchases for me. And, I believe that you value my opinion.*

T: *Why can't the motivation to shop with your wife just be love? If you know, she enjoys doing this and wants to share what she enjoys doing with the man she loves, and this should be enough motivation for him to spend this time with her.*

B: *First of all, playing the "if you love me, you will do this" card will not motivate your man to shop with you, and if he does, he won't enjoy it. However, love should be the motivating factor more than guilt or obligation. The desire to do something that your spouse will appreciate has its rewards.*

T: *Well, that's one way to look at it.*

B: I have to prepare myself every time we go out by recognizing it's your shopping time. Love may be the catalyst, but we still have to figure out how to enjoy the experience. Like shopping for that vintage sports car, tap into those same emotions and desires, and transfer that to shopping with your wife.

> ***Secret:*** *Dealing with the Gender issue: At some point, the male & female mindset meets but does not cross. Women and Men can relate to each other on various issues, but at some point, a man is a man, and a woman is a woman.*

CHAPTER 19
Commit To Your Commitments
Arabica Coffee House – Cleveland Heights, OH – 4 February 2004

Bobby: I hope this coffeehouse makes it. There's lots of competition in this area.

Tricia: Well, it has a nice ambiance about it; roomy, nice decor, and a fireplace.

B: They have free wi-fi; that's a plus. So, we were talking about commitment. Generally, in our society, when two people feel they are in love, they enter into a covenant of exclusivity with each other, which usually leads to marriage. That's what you do in our society; you get married. Even people who do not even desire marriage, after living together for a few years, experience societal pressure to validate their relationship with matrimony

T: So why don't they get married?

B: Yeah, why haven't couples like Oprah and Stedman married yet? They're undoubtedly monogamous.

T: How do you know that?

B: Please! Ok. They can't tip around. Where's she going to go and not be recognized? Where is he going to go?

T: So why don't people who seem committed to each other just get married?

B: Why do uncommitted people get married? They inevitably end up in divorce. Divorce breaks the marriage covenant. People don't want to enter into a covenant with God. Maybe that's it

T: That could be one of the reasons

B: Perhaps that's why they don't want to get married. They don't want to take those vows before God and enter into that covenant. It is rebellion, and rebellion is of the enemy.

T: That's true, that is so true.

B: The question still begs in my mind, why don't they, Oprah and Stedman, just get married? Again, it's a sign of rebellion. I believe that some people don't want to do what the Lord says to do. They feel it's a new thing for them. They think that cultural traditions of the past don't necessarily apply to them. So they try to set up new rules and create new cultures and practices, and isn't that one of the things the enemy does to get rid of God? Develop new cultures and new traditions that are without Him.

T: Yeah, but doesn't she considers herself a spiritual person

B: Why does she consider herself a spiritual person?

T: You can be spiritual and not be a Christian.

B: Exactly. But we're not talking about religion.

Some people are afraid to get married. They say, "if it ain't broke, don't mess with it. This relationship is working fine just like it is, so why get married and mess it up".

T: *Why do people think marriage will mess up the relationship?*

B: *Why, because now they have made a vow unto God that they feel they would have to honor it.*

T: *But they're honoring it already!*

B: *Not necessarily. In their relationship, they are. I think it goes deeper. Once again, like you just said, it's a trick of the enemy because you know what happens when you get married and take those vows before God?*

T: *You made a promise.*

B: *It's not just a promise; it's a spiritual thing that happens. Your souls meld into one. That's why divorce is like death. It's spiritual separation.*

T: *That's why people don't like things to change because there is a difference.*

B: *Like the verse of the Marriage Prayer that we have on our wall:*

"Dear Lord, please allow us to keep our distinctive personalities. Make us understand that what is good for our marriage is far more important than what is good for us as individuals." Your individuality is no longer the most important thing. People always say, "well, we're not married," which they believe excuses their behavior.

T: *Exactly*

B: *I don't want to do that. See, that's a trick. I admire Oprah and Stedman; I just believe they got it wrong.*

T: *(Laughs)*

B: *They're missing out on the next level. Marriage is a beautiful institution if you honor it and do it right. They're missing out. Maybe they will read the book.*

T: Well, maybe because they feel like the only thing they need is to have that love. We have love in our relationship.

B: But just having love in a relationship is a covenant with yourself, not God. It's parallel; it's not vertical.

T: Which is sufficient because now God blesses that union,

B: Which is the covenant. Why enter the covenant unless you want God to bless the marriage.

T: Exactly

> **Secret:** *Commit To Your Commitments. Do what you said you would, long after the mood you said it in has passed.*

CHAPTER 20
To Covenant...Or Not
Arabica Coffee House - Cleveland Heights, OH - 14 March 2004

Beyonce's song "Single Ladies" got everybody messed up. As the lyrics go, "If you like it, then you shoulda put a ring on it... Oh-oh-oh", and that's all that people did, put rings on it. It stopped at the engagement. They move in together, playing house. Many engaged couples reason that they'll live together while saving up money for the wedding sometime in the future. Still, the years fly by, and they're not married yet! I believe that this mega-hit song launched, or relaunched, a culture of cohabitation. Also commonly referred to as "Shacking Up." Don't they realize that Beyonce and Shawn Carter (Jay-Z) got married! Perhaps a sequel to the song would be in order with lyrics like "Put a ring on it- Then Get married... Oh-oh-oh!"

T: Marriage is between a man and a woman, making their vows before God.

B: The biblical definition of marriage is based on a covenant, which holds you accountable whether you intend to enter into it or not. God is faithful to his promises.

T: So the marriage institution itself falls under a covenant. Still, if you're not operating under God's laws and principles, you don't have the power to fulfill them.

B: Wouldn't that mean the power is present and available? Isn't that the key?

T: If you start operating in it

B: It's still there whether you operate in it or not

T: Then you don't have it

B: You have it; you don't use it. In the book "See you at the Top," Zig Ziglar tells the story of a man who does not utilize the available power at his disposal.

"Many years ago, oil was discovered on some Oklahoma property that belonged to an old man. He had been poverty-stricken all of his life, but the discovery of oil suddenly made him a very wealthy man. One of the first things he did was buy himself a big Cadillac touring car. Wanting the longest car in the territory, he added four more spare tires to the two already on the back. Every day he would drive into the hot, dusty, little Oklahoma town nearby. He wore an Abraham Lincoln stovepipe hat, tails, and a bow tie complete with a big black cigar. He would turn left and right, speaking to everyone in sight. Sometimes he would even turn all the way around without ever running into anybody or doing any physical or property damage. The reason is simple. Two horses were directly in front of that big beautiful automobile pulling it. Local mechanics said nothing was wrong with the engine, but the man never

switched on the ignition. Inside the car were a hundred horses ready, willing, and raring to go, but he was only using those two horses."

T: *No, I've never heard that story before.*

B: *Really, get out of here! This story goes back to marriage. All the brilliant things God will do if you align with His covenant; turn the key that links you to the power. But no, people want to stay hitched up to the horses (tradition); and remain in the flesh.*

T: *When I say flesh, I'm thinking of being in a carnal mind. That's why you now get all repercussions because you're not fulfilling your promises in the covenant. You have all these things that happen inside your marriage.*

B: *Just like divorce. Divorce is a death where people experience all the stages of grief. It's a spiritual separation of what God has put together. Whether they acknowledge it or not, they spiritually became one flesh.*

T: *Right*

B: *So it goes back to why people should not go into this thing haphazardly.*

T: *It's like what Bishop James Haughton used to always say when he married people, "You're entering into a covenant. You don't do this lightly. You do it reverently because you're doing it before God."*

B: *It's a wonder people don't seem to hear that. I remember Steve Harvey saying to me after church one day right before his first marriage that it was better to marry than to burn. (1 Corinthians 7:9 (AMP)*

T: *Because people enter into a marriage based on carnal motivations, meaning it's "how I feel about this person, it's what I feel we can do as a couple," it's all about them. It's not about what the marriage institution is. So when they operate in that mindset; you know, wow, we're going to have a wedding, we're getting married. We're going to do this and do that, and they leave God out of it; that's where the problems develop.*

B: *Exactly. Probably why the 50% divorce rate includes Christians and other religious people.*

T: *Even when they don't acknowledge God in a marriage, they can still have a successful marriage because the principles work.*

B: *You know why? Because God is faithful to His promises, to what He said He's going to do.*

T: *Right. He can still do that. But to those totally in the carnal mindset - the people who have rejected or twisted the bible because they marry or want to marry someone of the same sex are carnal-minded.*

B: *That's a chapter by itself. That's good stuff.*

T: *I recently heard Rev. Sharpton speak about this issue. He said, "I'm a reverend, and this whole talk that Pres. Bush is doing about using a constitutional amendment banning same-sex marriages is just a distraction. We've got to get to the other issues." And I'm saying, oh Brother Al, you're missing it. It is a big issue.*

B: *You know why he's missing it? Because politically, he's taking a democratic position. There's never been an amendment to the constitution that restricted rights.*

T: *And he's trying to say it's not a significant issue compared to jobs or whether the country will be at war, but it is. It establishes a base for how we operate when we get into that family unit.*

B: *Do you agree with President Bush putting this in the constitution?*

T: *I think there has to be a moral stand to say we will not let carnal-minded immoral people push those things down our throats. It's like the devil.*

B: *That's a reasonable response; now, answer my question, do you agree it should be in the constitution?*

T: *Not really. I don't believe you can effectively legislate morality.*

B: *And why would it have to be amended to the constitution? It's already written in the word.*

T: *Why did they have to put in the constitution that all men are created equal?*

B: *Now that's a good point. So just banning it is not enough.*

T: *What happens from state to state is that people will want to do their own thing. You have to do something for the country, the nation, that will be the same. Otherwise, people in their states will do whatever they want to do. Ok. But yeah, I believe that some order is necessary.*

B: *What's blowing my mind is how many folks are coming out and doing this same-sex marriage thing. That's why what we're doing is so important. We have to talk about the challenging issues; otherwise, we're just doing a fluff piece.*

T: *Right, we can't skirt around them. Not in our book.*

> **Secret:** *Can you have a covenant with yourself, or does the covenant require a relationship? Entering into a covenant requires accountability, assessment, and responsibility—horizontal covenants with other people, vertical covenants with God.*

CHAPTER 21
Let's Talk About Sex
Magic Johnson's Starbucks - Cleveland Heights, OH - Sunday, 5 June 2005

B: *Tonight, let's talk about sex. A little sizzle here.*

T: *Ok, that's an important topic, especially when committing to a marriage.*

B: *It's an important topic when you're talking about life! Any relationship between male and female. I mean, even now, the whole sex thing is blurred.*

T: *Ultimately, our focus is on marriage, so I guess the worldly view of sex would interfere with a marital view or because of worldly influences.*

B: *The last I heard, the divorce rate was 60% in this country, with a large part of that being in the church. You still have the issues of sex, money & politics.*

T: *Politics?*

B: *Or sex, drugs, rock & roll; either way you shake it, sex is prominently involved. Sex is a vital component of marriage. It's a critical part of the instability. Last night, you said in the Davidic study you're doing how that lifestyle was his downfall and his son Solomon's downfall. It was sex. I always wondered why it was acceptable for a king to have multiple partners?*

T: *Yes, it was. Even though it's something that men do, it's not the norm.*

B: *As I said before, it's not just something men do; women also. That's the other side of the equation. Yeah, but I'm talking about that higher libido thing. That's true. So if somebody asked you, you know, how is your sex life? What would you say?*

T: *(Chuckling) Uh, that's a good question; it tells a lot.*

B: *Thank you very much. That's what you would say to women, or what you're saying to me? I'm that somebody.*

T: *Um, I would say it's not as good as I would want it to be, but better than it has been.*

B: *Oh! You'll have to elaborate on that. Not as good as you would want it to be, but better than it has been? Man, that is so layered; let's start pulling away some of those layers. I would like to have more zest; I guess, a zeal for physical (trails off)*

T: *Intimacy? Yeah, and what keeps me from that is my physical; it's how I feel, you know, not feeling well. That interferes a great deal with it.*

B: *Well, health is a big deal with sex, and you know that goes into the commitment of a relationship.*

T: *Yeah.*

B: *Because if your relationship is built just on the sexual experience, our sexual experience has been, from, you know, just incredible to frustrating.*

T: *Yeah.*

B: *You know, I mean, just certain heights have been crazy fantastic*

T: *Yeah, I want more*

B: *It was such a source of frustration during our younger years. That's why our commitment to each other had to transcend just the physical. Most people know that intuitively, but there's such an innate need for the physical component.*

T: *Well, that I believe*

B: *What happens then if something goes wrong physically? Then outside influences and opportunities for intimate outlets present themselves. That's when infidelity occurs.*

T: *Like Dr. Phil says, "how's that working for you?" With a divorce rate of 60%, I think it's not ok.*

B: *But you have to look at what part of that is because of sex*

T: *I think a large amount of that is because of sex.*

B: *Get out of here!*

T: *Sex and or finances are the two biggest things. Those are the Twin Towers.*

B: *But you know what, it's more than that because then the sex becomes a band-aide that you're putting on to cover another problem, a bigger problem. It's not that. It's something people do to either forget something painful,*

T: *You mean sex?*

B: *Yeah, sometimes that's what it is; they do that because they don't want to deal with other issues, then they make it into that, but I don't think it starts out being that, and I don't believe that's the real reason.*

Tricia:

Circa 2020

There are lean years and fat years like any other season in a marriage or relationship. Sexual intimacy in the fat years is a fun adventure. Enjoy the fat years. If you are not intentional in wanting to keep it vibrant, you will quickly develop habits that will damage your sex life and your bond as a couple. When we chose to grow in this area, our love blossomed, even when the act of lovemaking was not there.

It is essential to know that satisfying lovemaking increases the frequency of sexual intimacy. So what happens to couples to change this? Life. It was paramount to recognize that changes in our sex life came hand in hand with changes in our life. If you are together, as long as we are, there are a lot of changes. Physical intimacy may or may not include sexual intercourse in every encounter.

Health issues, children, workplace challenges, financial stress, and whatever life throws at you. These life situations will test a marriage and can create lean years if we do not communicate our needs and limitations with our partners. Sexual intimacy is even more important in these times. It can be achieved with grace and mutual respect for our partner.

Let's distinguish between sex and physical intimacy. The act itself is only part of physical intimacy. Oftentimes, however, it seems to get the most focus. I believe people develop harmful expectations that are shaped by cultural influences, pornography, and abuse. Cultural influences range from sex being something we do as entertainment to exploring fantasies influenced by music and other media.

Bobby and I love each other. This love challenges me and grows my desire to please him. He does the same for me. We have a growing sexual attraction for one another that makes us guard our physical intimacy. The two of us have decided what that is for us and not the culture.

> ***Secret:*** *Consistent, mutually satisfying physical intimacy will strengthen your marriage. Self-sabotaging behaviors can develop long-term intimacy problems in relationships.*

CHAPTER 22
Rebirth Of Inspiration

South Euclid, OH – circa 2011

Life had gotten in the way; the manuscript lay dormant, the project discarded. It was a time of intense struggles. I had substantial financial setbacks and personal doubts and was suffering from depression. I was stuck and looking for a way out, struggling for a spark of motivation.

Microsoft Words was about to begin charging a fee. My son Dorjän suggested that I transfer my files to the free LibreOffice. I did not want to incur any additional expenses, so I forced myself into my home office to transfer the files. That was when I ran across the abandoned manuscript drafts from years ago. As I was reading through the stories and the coffee shop conversations, I saw a glimpse of the person I used to be. That adventurous and bold individual full of life and enthusiasm, ready to take on the world and accomplish great things. Somewhere along the way, I lost that confidence, expectancy, and that fire!

The last recession all but wiped us out financially. Also, I decided to give up the home-based business ventures that had occupied my time and dreams for so many years. Perhaps it was just fading youthfulness, but I felt aged. I knew somehow I needed to get back to my former self.

Hope deferred makes the heart sick, but a dream fulfilled is a tree of life. Proverbs 13:12 (NLT)

This was my moment of pause, of clarity from the fog that had engulfed me. Why not be forever young, at least in mind and spirit! I had gotten lost in the circumstances of life and was not being true to who I was, just who I thought I had become. This was indeed my "physician, heal thyself" moment.

Those pages took me back to my foundation of positivity and my pursuit of excellence. They motivated me to begin my road to recovery. I had stretched out this self-pity party long enough. I constructed a new plan and dream and started writing again with renewed faith and enthusiasm.

PART IV
ANNIVERSARIES: *THE RELATIONSHIP OPTIMIZATION TOOL*

CHAPTER 23
Monthly Celebrations:
The Relationship Optimization Tool

Tricia and I were just teenagers in the infantile stages of first love. What began as youthful exuberance has become our most effective *Relationship Optimization Tool: The Monthly Couple Anniversary*. We started going together (became an exclusive couple) on November 2nd, 1971, and acknowledged every month since. Sometimes at midnight, we just turn to each other in bed, say "Happy Anniversary," then go back to sleep. Other times, it involved large bouquets of balloons representing each month. A spontaneous getaway trip to a quaint Bed & Breakfast, romantic dinners, and hundreds of anniversary cards. Someone recently asked me the question as to how long we have been together? It was fun to reply, "three hundred ninety-eight months," it's a different perspective. We recommend a monthly check-in with each other to keep your relationship on track for success and happiness.

Relationships need periodic maintenance like our laptops, smartphones, and automobiles to keep them running at peak performance. Likewise, it requires a focused and determined effort to achieve and maintain a successful, loving, and long-term relationship. While it is important to remember and celebrate anniversaries, they tend to lose their impact because they are too far apart. A monthly celebration encourages your focus on the incremental adjustments needed to maintain optimal performance or success.

We instinctively knew that concentrating on celebrating our monthly anniversary of becoming a couple was essential to our longevity and success. Years later, we discovered the practice of Neuro-Linguistic Programming (NLP), popularized by Tony Robbins, the world-renowned strategist. We learned that our monthly focus gave us a periodic check-up and put us into "State," taking us back to that fateful day when Tricia segued from hesitancy to certainty, and we became a couple. We again become those 16 and 17-year-olds that fall in love with each other.

> ***Secret:*** *Time is an invaluable gift; use it wisely. Always finding reasons to celebrate is a good idea! Use anniversaries as a checkup to assess the health of your relationship.*

What Is Your 'State'?

In 1994, we took a trip to New York City to break in our first new car. We played the album "Street Player" by Rufus & Chaka Khan for the entire trip on the 8-track player to anchor the experience. Years later, when we hear songs like "Stay" or "Street Player," it transports us back to the 19 and

20-year-olds in that car driving the streets of Times Square and Midtown Manhattan. Once again, we feel the energy, the sounds, and the smells that engulf us. We were determined that we would not be the typical tourists depicted in the movies, walking around New York and staring into the skies. We were doing pretty good playing it cool until we got stuck in traffic. We could no longer contain ourselves, so we threw open our doors and stood in the street in amazement, looking up, gawking at the skyscrapers, then laughed like crazy at our lack of conviction.

For years, we intuitively anchored our experiences to music but it wasn't until the trip to New York that we did it intentionally, with forethought. That was also the trip when Dorjän was conceived. How's that for a state!

> **Secret:** *"Take control of your consistent emotions and begin to consciously and deliberately reshape your daily experience of life." – Tony Robbins*

CHAPTER 24
The 25th Wedding Anniversary
Mt. Sinai Baptist Church – Cleveland, OH – April 2003

Tricia:

The Black Marriage Day initiative began in 2002 to create a cultural shift in the black community in how we view and celebrate marriage. We were honored to renew our wedding vows as part of the first ceremony held in Cleveland.

Our marriage was destiny. God honors the commitment of a man and woman in marriage. After creating the heavens and the earth was God's creation of man. After man, woman. God made a woman comparable to a man. Marriage is the covenant commitment between the two. The deception of Eve caused the first instance of Satan's influence on the marriage covenant.

Our marriage is blessed because our spirits, hearts, and minds align with God's Spirit. God has set our souls in the same orbit. Our marriage is becoming the image of this holy unit God has preordained. What interferes with

God's vision of marriage is allowing Satan to create enmity between husbands and wives. If we are to remain faithful and not fail in our commitment and covenant to each other, we must keep God as the head. Honoring God is what keeps the marriage thriving.

We planted a seed of faith on our wedding day. We were trusting in the covenant commitment of marriage. Twenty-five years later, our marriage has become the fruit of that seed. A fruit that is still sweet and delicious, producing the seeds of new life and commitment to each other. Our life is like two plants grafted to form a new life. Stronger than the individual plant, each is contributing to its fortitude.

Our marriage is a witness to God's gift of man to woman and woman to man. My husband is God's gift to me every day. I believe blessings will continue to flow significantly through our marriage to create not just new life but new testimony to the faithfulness of God to His creation. We cannot fail in our commitment to each other because we have chosen not to forget God.

God's covenant is a covenant of relationship. A husband and a wife who does not honor this relationship leave room for dissent and transgression. We are about to take our relationship to a new place.

CHAPTER 25
The 26th Wedding Anniversary

Coffee Conversation
Magic Johnson's Starbucks – Cleveland Heights, OH – 3 May 2004

B: Today, we're celebrating our 389th MonthlyCoupleVersary and our 26th wedding anniversary weekend!

T: Oh, yeah [chuckling]

B: I think about how we celebrate every month. Sometimes we just turn over in bed and say "happy anniversary," then go back to sleep, still acknowledging the day. I think something unusual happened yesterday

T: I know, we didn't exchange presents or cards.

B: Exactly! Now, why is that? Did you think about it? I know you didn't forget, so what was your thought process for not giving me a present or a card?

T: I don't know if I had a thought process. It wasn't something I felt I needed to do this time.

B: Do you think that's a negative precedent, that we're so comfortable with each other that we don't see a need to acknowledge it with a card or something?

T: No, that wasn't it at all.

B: I mean, I'm culpable; I didn't give you anything either. I thought about it; I just didn't.

T: Right. I think I felt that too; it wasn't necessary to do it.

B: Why is that? Why wasn't it necessary? Cause people, you know, go to war over something like this. We go to war over something like this.

T: [laughing]... Well, not war.

B: Well, you know, we've gone through some emotions concerning this stuff

T: Not really

B: Yeah, we have. Need I remind you about that particular Christmas?

T: Ok, but that's not an anniversary.

B: Anniversaries, all right. So what do you think?

T: We knew we would spend time together; that was sufficient.

B: Like an unspoken mutual agreement.

T: (chuckles) Sometimes, we do tell if we're going to give cards or not.

B: Well, yes, but that always felt kind of weird.

T: Weird?

B: Yes, because I'm not going to get you a card just because you're going to get me one.

T: You say that, not me.

B: Right, I do say it is weird, so I don't say it anymore.

T: *I think celebrating an anniversary is essential to mark the day.*

B: *We celebrate every single month*

T: *Right*

B: *Not just because we've done it since high school; it's a high point, a tuneup.*

T: *Ok*

B: *I've pushed the monthly anniversary thing much more than you have.*

T: *Right, but we've done it long enough that it's not something I'll forget.*

B: *I think it's a beautiful thing. I love our relationship; I love our marriage. I think we should always pause to celebrate.*

T: *That is why they are beneficial. Now, how you choose to observe that day is a matter of taste and personal preference. Just as long as you don't make light of it because that's when people sometimes get in trouble.*

B: *What do you mean, make light?*

T: *Some people acknowledge that it's their anniversary, and some totally forget.*

B: *Yep, you've got to concentrate and set aside the time. Sometimes, it's fun just to count the months.*

T: *We've counted the days too.*

B: *Well yeah, but after like 270 months, we're beyond the days. Remember when I rented a helium tank, and the kids and I blew all those balloons up. Was it an anniversary or your birthday?*

T: *It was my birthday, I think.*

B: There were a lot of balloons. All the kids forgot our wedding anniversary that year, except for Seneca.

T: He's usually the one who doesn't remember stuff like that.

B: Jonathan says, "you guys have so many anniversaries I get confused." [both chuckle] We live out the example of celebrating our relationship, our marriage before our children.

T: Not only that, many times, people only acknowledge the landmarks like five years, ten years, that kind of thing. The ones that fall in-between, say the 11th year are not big deals.

B: Yeah, but that's kind of a cop-out, just remembering the mile-stone anniversary; every one of them is significant. The thing that happens to many relationships is that they barely mark off the years, and time just rolls by, but their relationship is not in a good place. It's deteriorating, and they don't know what to do. They're not happy and probably want to leave the relationship.

T: Their anniversary is not a cause for celebration, but a reminder of making a mistake and ending up with who they think is the wrong person. That could be why some people don't mark anniversaries. In their private way, they know they're not celebrating.

B: Right. Would I marry you all over again? Now that's an excellent check-up question. Would you marry your spouse again right now?

T: If you can't say yes, what's going on in that relationship?

B: You tell yourself that another month has passed; what am I doing with my life? Why am I still here?

T: Right, it's like you said, a check-up.

B: Celebration and check-up.

T: It's also a point of renewal and recommitment. The most important thing about anniversaries is not just the fun of celebrating them; the joy is reliving the feelings, attitudes, and emotions of the day you married or began the relationship with that person. Revisiting those feelings and emotions helps to renew and strengthen you. That's why people renew their vows because they want to return to that feeling at that moment. After all, a relationship goes through many emotional ups and downs.

B: It's the materialization of the thought that I would marry you all over again. The whole thing about renewing vows is a misnomer, going back to making a vow, renewing a covenant just to make it fresh, but if it's not broken, why renew it?

T: No, it's not broken.

B: So why renew it. Why go through all of that?

T: Okay, think about when the Lord specifically told the Jews to remember certain events and even how to remember them. Why did He give them a specific way to remember an event?

B: Part of that, I think, is because when you remember that event, you pass along the essence of that event to the next generation because they didn't live that event

T: Right, doing that in front of your children lets them share an event they were not privy to because they weren't born or old enough to remember. There is also symbolism involved. So renewing is making something fresh.

B: Ok.

T: You're getting a fresh dose and creating in your mind a certain awakening point, which, in a sense, is spiritual.

B: Recommitting

T: Sometimes, people have all of these ideas about how they want to celebrate their anniversary and mark the occasion. When they're not able to do it that way, they get disappointed. They think they have to spend a lot of money because it's a big occasion.

B: I agree. That reminds me of what I tell people when I shoot a wedding, "What happens on the wedding day, happens on the wedding day." You can plan stuff to the nth degree, and something unexpected will arise. You have to deal with it. You have to keep your attitude in check, handle it and move on.

CHAPTER 26
Our 552nd MonthlyCoupleVersary
The Red Maple Inn - Chardon, OH - Thursday, 2 November 2017

We kicked off the weekend festivities with a tour of our high school. The building underwent extensive interior renovations and exterior restoration. We got turned around inside but finally got our bearings by sitting in the auditorium where we used to meet every day before classes. We wrapped up the visit with a selfie photo session outside the school. Afterward, we headed out to the Hard Rock Rocksino for a light dinner before seeing Kirk Franklin and Ledisi in concert. And yes, it was a gospel concert in a casino!

The following day we took a relaxing drive out of the city to Amish country to spend a couple of days at the Red Maple Inn. We talked about starting a podcast after publishing the book. So, after walking through the hallways of our high school, reminiscing, we turned our focus to plans for the future. This is a perfect example of how the Relationship Optimization Tool is a vital asset to success as a couple.

The Bible says in Psalm 84:7 that "we grow from strength to strength." Remembering the foundational recurring events in your relational history often inspires the subsequent memories you create together.

Join the conversation:
- What is your focus when you celebrate your anniversary?
  - Are you concentrating on the current plans to celebrate?
  - Or, are you taking a memory journey to that special day it happened?
- How did you celebrate your last anniversary?
- What other occasions in your relationship do you celebrate? (i.e., first kiss, first date, etc.)

Some ideas for celebrating anniversaries:
- Keeping a promise that you made, no matter how long ago you made it
- Write a love letter or note to each other
- Making love in a different location than ever before
- Return to the venue of your first date
- Get a couples mani-pedi and or a couples massage, etc.
  - Spa
  - Bed & Breakfast
  - Resort
- Cook a meal together
  - Plan & shop together
  - Order meal delivery (Blue Apron, Home Chef, etc)
- Take a professional photo

- Adopt a puppy
- Attending a marriage/relationship conference (ie, Weekend to Remember, Whole Bean the Experience (working title)
- Learn something new together
- Create a T-shirt for the occasion wear it to talk about your love for each other when people comment on your relationship
- Travel and experience a new place
- Do an activity you've never done before
    - Hot Air Balloon Ride
    - Jet Ski
    - Skydive
    - Sailing Lessons
    - Take a Cruise
    - Ballroom dance lessons
    - Scuba diving lessons
    - Take a race car driving course
    - Bike ride tour across Europe or Viet Nam etc.
    - Motorcycle riding course
    - Rent and ride scooters all-day
    - Watch a beautiful sunset together, embracing the Zen method
    - Parasailing (something for us to do!)
    - Create a family crest

PART V
RELATIONAL FISSURES: *MOMENTS OF CRISIS*

CHAPTER 27
Enter stooping down
Cleveland, OH – February 1979

My dad served in World War II as an Army Master Sergeant. He ran our household like he was still in the service. It was always "yes sir" and "no sir." He would often share his philosophy with my siblings and me about growing up and preparing to leave home. He would reference the side door (the main entrance) and tell us that our preparation for success in the world started here at home. Adult life begins once we leave out of that door. The door metaphor was akin to his idea of what it takes "To be a man."

The first time I 'left out of that door' was a quiet event. I was moving into my first apartment and starting a family. I was employed, bought my first new car, and attended art school and community college. The second time was with much fanfare. I was a newly married man embarking on a grand international adventure.

I have not lived at home for over five years. Coming back home, back through that side door, was devastating. With my wife in tow, well pregnant with our 2nd child and our 3-year-old son, I felt like I was shrinking, my life totally out of control, stooping down just to fit. Chased out of Iran with little more than the baggage we could carry, we had few choices of where to live. I am grateful that my folks took us in.

It will take a few years until I finally come to terms with the events during this time. They had blueprinted deep-set enmity and misplaced aggression in my life. I unjustly focused my disappointments on my 2nd child, Seneca, subconsciously blaming him for the death of my international dreams.

I thank God that I finally recognized and resolved this issue before the domino effect caused irreparable damage to our relationship.

CHAPTER 28
Interrupting The Domino Effect

Have you ever seen the World Championship Domino Tournament? It's an exciting and fast-paced event. The competition begins when the contestants push their first domino. This chip starts a chain reaction of tumbling tiles moving at tremendous speeds, spreading to multiple rows, clicking and falling simultaneously, thus causing the "Domino Effect," when one event sets off a chain of similar events.

I was watching the competition when something happened that caught my attention. A misspaced domino failed to connect, effectively stopping the anticipated next event from occurring. The chain reaction had come to a dead stop. The contestant had to carefully go over the standing domino that the previous tile had missed and manually push it to begin the action again. No doubt, taking advantage of the interruption to assess the remaining line's proper spacing before proceeding.

So why not apply this to real-life conflicts? At any point, someone can step up and deliberately stop the Domino

Effect (the series of events triggering adverse circumstances) before the altercation or the argument further deteriorates the situation. But accomplishing this is no easy task, especially in the heat of the moment when escalating emotions have replaced rational reasoning. One party must step up, recognize the cascading pattern, then take action before the situation spirals completely out of control.

> *"Like apples of gold in settings of silver is a word spoken at the right time."* Proverbs 25:11 (AMP)

Prearranging the following sequence in advance is imperative, especially within the confines of intimate relationships. This strategic interference allows all parties to interrupt the downward spiral and cultivate an amicable resolution:

#1. Someone has to interrupt the flow of events.

#2. Stop. Just Stop — Take a deep breath — Calm yourself.

#3. Assess the situation — Acknowledge the Domino Effect, the Negative Spiral

#4. Agree together on the best resolution (strategy) for this situation.

#5. Together agree to operate in this new line of resolve moving forward.

Secret: *An affectionate gesture interrupts a negative flow*

Tricia and I had an opportunity to apply the *Domino Effect Interruption* philosophy to our son Seneca's dilemma in middle school. We had gotten adverse reports from some of his teachers. Seneca was a brilliant student, so this news gave us cause for concern. We discovered that this undue scrutiny from his teachers resulted from Seneca befriending a young man at his school who was always in trouble. Seneca was not causing any problems himself, but some teachers assumed him guilty by association. I was livid! How dare they place these unfounded accusations on my son? These people had effectively pushed my (domino) button, and they were about to get a piece of my mind! Tricia became that "definitive pause" for me (Step #1). From that state of calmness (#2), we established our strategy (#4) for a positive outcome.

- Affirm Seneca for his decision to remain faithful to his friends regardless of undue pressure.
- Isolate Seneca from the other students' actions to his teachers and school administrators.
- We created a document for the teachers to fill out daily that would only take a few minutes to complete. It consisted of a checklist for behavior with a comment section at the end.,
- We set up a meeting of all his teachers and the vice-principal at the school, requesting that each teacher fill out and sign this document after each class for two weeks.
- We would check the report every night and send it back to the teacher the next day.
- This process would provide multiple outcomes:
- It would force the teacher to focus only on Seneca's attitude, performance, and behavior that day, eliminating their bias or prejudices based on socialization.

- Seneca would benefit from knowing that he was being evaluated solely for his performance and not his associations with other students. Thus, preventing him from spiraling into a negative mindset.
- Allows Tricia and me to monitor each classroom and provides us with documentation of any implicit bias if that should be the case.

The exercise was a total success. Seneca's teachers evaluated him on his own merits and behavior and stopped the adverse reporting. One educator, the main culprit of the profiling, was so impressed that she asked permission to use our report for all of her classes.

CHAPTER 29
The Storm: *Marriage in Chaos*

The Reconstruction Period: Starting Over
Cleveland, OH Area - Saturday, 26 September 2015

We argued first thing this morning. It was my fault, really; Tricia had just had enough. Then, we had another one in the afternoon, again, my fault. After dropping her off to care for her mom, I went to Wade Oval, my favorite creative place. I was sitting in one of the Adirondack chairs under the big tree, watching a lovely autumn evening wedding. Tricia said, "You're killing me. I was angry and was taking it out on her." It's true. Since I have not worked or earned significant income for a while now, our financial picture is bleak. I was "robbing Peter to pay Paul," doing my best to make ends meet. Keeping her in the dark about our situation, at least until I can figure a way out of this.

Meanwhile, Tricia worked and taught school in a stressful setting, and I was not helping. She said, "All this while being a Christian man, I do not understand." She's right; I guess I am angry, definitely disappointed.

It is such a conflicting moment watching this couple start their married life together while we are — at this exact moment — finding our marriage in such jeopardy. Do they know what they're getting themselves into? Something inside me wanted to shout, "don't do it!" That thought alone was heartbreaking, so I countered my negativity by submitting a prayer for them. They broke the glass to a round of applause, Mazel Tov! There is still hope.

Putting On A Good Face
New Community Bible Fellowship – Sunday, 27 September 2015

Pastor Kevin and sister Tanya slowly walked to the front of the church as I followed them in my role as armor-bearer to attend to him during the second service. I still felt the weight of the previous day's argument with Tricia and was at my station purely out of duty, but with the rawness and subjectivity of wanting and needing to hear what God would say to me this morning. Yesterday's events laid me wide open. I was reeling, reevaluating my values and where my focus had been over these past few years. Was I challenging my faith? Was I having doubts and seeking something else, something more? I was determined to find out and find out today!

Self Talk
Monday, 5 October 2015

Last night I had a breakthrough. I asked myself the question: What is a successful marriage? That is the question, is it not? My focus is on thriving. Tricia said, "We are not thriving at all." Finances are at the top of the list for reasons of marriage failure. Not just the lack thereof, but research shows that even when financial resources are abundant, there is a failure without a balance of communication and full disclosure. Was I really protecting her from stress, or am I just trying to wait it out and cover myself? Perhaps I had the right intentions but did it the wrong way.

Tricia:

Keeping secrets in a relationship is like black holes. Not the success secrets that we're referencing throughout the book, but the things couples keep hidden from each other. The gravitational pull is so strong that nothing can escape. Maintaining these types of secrets requires tremendous energy. Secrets in a marriage or serious relationships bring dark and obtrusive shadows that become an entity hiding, pieces of a soul that do not reflect its pure light. This shadow grows into an ever-widening crevice that begins to separate you from your partner and from yourself. This chasm will eventually swallow one or both of you with no way out. They will ultimately be exposed as bitterness, anxiety, depression, overcompensation, or mistrust. Come clean. Trust in a relationship is light.

> **Secret:** *Come clean. Project your future. Do you value the person and relationship so much that your future is less without them? Do you both see the other person as viable for your future? Marriage is not just a financial decision.*

CHAPTER 30
Deserts, Mountaintops, Peaks, and Valleys

These were low, humbling, pivotal times. The vicissitudes of life found us traversing barren and hardened desert landscapes, desperate to find the waters of release. But, we persevered, surveyed our position, then focused on shoring up the foundations and the pillars on which we built our faith and marriage. We planted the seeds in that fertile and rich topsoil, found only on the valley floor of despair. New roots will flourish by watering and supplying the proper nutrients, pulling the weeds as they spring up to choke the new growth.

The peaks and mountaintops are difficult places to learn; there is no growth on the top of a mountain. But these are the times when you experience your best joy. Lean in, grow and cherish these precious moments. Make them last; it is a beautiful time in life and should be guarded, enjoyed, and celebrated.

Tricia:

I knew Bobby had been struggling for a while. Both of us felt the business disappointments. I knew the work he had put into making his entrepreneurial dreams come true, and I was heartbroken for him. But the bills do not stop while you are building. You have to make the hard decisions to do what is necessary.

Men don't always share their struggles with doubt and depression. If we had communicated more about what was going on, things would have been different. I believed our foundation was strong, but it was becoming shaky. I am one to think that tough times require tough choices. I felt like I was making the tough choices to do what was needed, and Bobby was not doing the same. I felt betrayed because he made decisions in isolation. Isolation is the enemy of marriage. The good soil of our marriage, communication, faith, trust, and loyalty had eroded to blaming and shaming. We were both guilty of this, especially me. I didn't see my husband struggling; I saw him as someone who didn't care how his choices affected our family. I became indifferent to the point of having no feelings for him. Yes, I prayed. I cried out to God. Yes, God heard me. He sustained me long enough for change to come.

> ***Secret:*** *You have to focus on the promise more than the problem*

In a marriage, you will not always be able to see how the trial will turn out; you may not have even seen it coming. We could never have imagined that our working honeymoon to Iran would end up as it did. It became our proving ground. We stayed focused on honoring our promise to our marriage and our family. This was our true North. Things worked in our favor when we focused on the promise more than the problems. God honored our commitment to our marriage.

Let's continue the conversation. We would love to hear from you. www.TheCoffeeCouple.org

CONCLUSION

Approximately 10,000 people have been passengers in my car during my first three years of ride-sharing for Uber and Lyft. I stopped driving people in early 2021 because of the onset of COVID-19 in the U.S. Given the opportunity, I would reference the longevity of Tricia's and my relationship, usually followed by the question: "What's your secret?" It didn't matter if they were 16 years old or 45; the inquiry was the same. After probing them for personal background information, I responded: *Communication, Communication, Communication.*

Ask a real estate broker what the best predictor of a successful business venture is, and the usual response is *Location, Location, Location*. Similarly, *Communication*³ holds equal importance in experiencing a successful long-term relationship and or marriage. The question remains: How does one effectively communicate to their partner, and how can you make sure they understand what you're trying to say or do?

The following allegory, although perhaps not in the best of taste, exhibits effective communication:

A couple whose domestic tranquility had long been the talk of the town were celebrating their golden wedding anniversary. A local newspaper reporter was inquiring about the secret of their long and happy marriage. "Well, it dates back to our honeymoon," explained the wife. "We visited the Grand Canyon and took a trip down to the bottom by pack mule. We hadn't gone too far when my husband's mule stumbled. My husband quietly said, "That's Once." We proceeded a little farther when the mule stumbled again. Once more, my husband quietly said, "That's Twice." We hadn't gone a half-mile when the mule stumbled a third time. My husband took a pistol from his pocket and shot him dead. I started to protest over his treatment of the mule when he looked at me and quietly said, "That's Once."... Anonymous

Just a little side note, my wife does not like this story. It is an outdated old-world reference, but I believe it makes the point. The story is also told from the husband's voice, where the wife is the perpetrator. That version usually ends with the husband saying, "And from that moment.....we have lived happily ever after."

Effective communication between couples is when one party hears (not just listens) and understands what the other party is saying. The goal should be mutual understanding, like in the movie Rush Hour when Chris Tucker's character says to Jackie Chan's character, "Do you understand the words that are coming out of my mouth?"

Some would contend that communication is only a matter of talking and listening. That opinion would fail to realize that effective communication involves specific skills that can be learned and developed. There is a plethora of information available on this subject. It's a wise couple who venture into this research together.

Let us give you a head start. Tricia and I have subscribed to Dr. Gary Chapman's "The Five Love Languages." We have taken the Love Language Quiz several times over many years to better communicate with each other. We have developed a little twist to the quiz that made the exercise even more effective for us. You can get it on our website:

www.TheCoffeeCouple.org

Sometimes, even the best intentions for effective communication are based on assumptions, leading to unnecessary conflicts. But even those arguments have value, as long as the proper boundaries are established. Learn to argue eloquently. Our years together have proven that one way to prolong and increase the volatility of an argument is for one party to walk away unless by mutual agreement to take a cooling-off period before coming back to the table at an agreed time. Otherwise, this "exit" only continues the downward spiral of the domino effect.

We have done our best to live out the biblical advice in our relationship: "Don't let the sun go down on your wrath," Ephesians 4:26. But there have been many times when this strategy was not achievable. Those were the long nights when we embraced the sage wisdom of the American stand-up comedian, actress, and author Phylis Diller when she said, "Never go to bed mad. Stay up and fight!"

EPILOGUE

Marriage Is The Ultimate Romantic Relationship. A successful relationship and marriage environment promotes a healthier society for us all.

God created, ordained, and blessed the institution of marriage, but He did not make it mandatory to believe in Him to be married.

Even though we did not fully unpack this concept in these writings, we plan a deep dive into this matter in a future project. Perhaps another book or a podcast.

But for now, we express our deepest gratitude and sincere appreciation to you for allowing us to share a bit of our journey.

With this in mind, we offer you this closing prayer until our paths cross again.

A Marriage Prayer

"Dear Lord, we ask that you give our marriage a special blessing that will help and guide us in our lives together as man and wife.
Lord, we ask that ours be a marriage of equality, a marriage where neither overshadows the other, a marriage where success and achievements are equally shared with the faults and failures.
Dear Lord, please allow us to keep our individual personalities, but make us understand that what is good for our marriage is far more important than what is good for us as individuals. Lord, bless us with the patience and wisdom to understand one another, the strength to support each other, the compassion it takes to say, "I'm sorry", and the love to forgive. Amen"

THE AUTHORS

***If I am the philosopher in our relationship,
then Tricia is the pragmatist; I am, so she must be***

Patricia is a retired educator with years of experience with children and families, and she has seen (all too often) how divorce negatively impacts both. She feels that by making marriages and relationships strong, you shore up the family and help children do better in life. Her work with families and children as a wraparound specialist propels her desire to help people build nurturing and healthy relationships. She has spoken to women's groups about marriage and has been a facilitator for small groups in the church.

Bobby is an accomplished, internationally traveled professional photographer. Exhibited by his photography and network marketing background, he has a critical eye for detail and analysis of information. Bobby has led several small groups at his local church and served as an adjunct to the senior pastor. As an entrepreneur, he has vast experience in training, sales, and marketing.

For the last 50 years, their lives have centered around one romantic relationship driven by a passionate focus on the pursuit of excellence. Their first book, Whole Bean the Marriage Blend, focuses on their life together, from high school sweethearts to their marriage of over 44 years. The ability to share the 'Secrets for Success,' derived from their life experiences, along with a great cup of coffee, is a must-read for anyone desiring a Successfully Thriving and Loving Relationship.

Keep in touch with The Coffee Couple:

Facebook: https://www.facebook.com/rl.scott
Instagram: https://www.instagram.com/triciascott_02/
https://www.instagram.com/bobby_l_scott/
Website: www.TheCoffeeCouple.org

www.ingramcontent.com/pod-product-compliance
Lightning Source LLC
LaVergne TN
LVHW012021060526
838201LV00061B/4404